The GIFT Within YOU

by

Dr. R. Lattier, Ph.D.

The Gift Within You

Published by:

McDougal & Associates
18896 Greenwell Springs Road
Greenwell Springs, LA 70739
www.ThePublishedWord.com

McDougal & Associates is dedicated to the spreading of the Gospel of Jesus Christ to as many people as possible in the shortest time possible.

ISBN 978-1-940461-39-7

Printed on demand in the US, the UK and Australia
For Worldwide Distribution

"It's your session to create and shine for Me," says the Lord. Relax and watch me do it!

Dedication

To Adina Joy, my loving wife of forty plus years, I dedicate this book.

Dr. R. [illegible]

Acknowledgements

I thank God and the countless individuals, like my father and twin daughters, who have inspired me to write this book. I also thank my friend Carol who made it financially possible.

Contents

Every desirable and beneficial gift comes out of heaven. The gifts are rivers of light cascading down from the Father of Light. There is nothing deceitful in God, nothing two-faced, nothing fickle.

James 1:17

Introduction

You were born with a gift from God. God made you with this unique gift to bless the world and all humanity. There will never be another person like you!

Your gift has defined you since childhood. It was always present and active. Perhaps you did not understand it nor have a name for it, but it was there deep inside of you. It was your gift, and you believed that everyone had it, but they did not. You knew, you saw and you heard things that others did not.

The gift you have is to be shared with others. God never intended it to be a personal ego trip. God chose your gift. Your gift is exactly the one that God had in mind for you. It's a perfect match to your personality and natural talents.

Actually, everything about you complements your gift. The family you were born into, for example, enhanced your gift. Whether you had siblings or not was all designed for that gift you carry. The time, the location and the surroundings of your birth and childhood were all planned with your gift in mind. Only God could orchestrate in harmony all those events for you.

Life becomes meaningful when you discover your gift. It's like that hidden piece of a puzzle which is found to finish the picture. Now you can see clearly and understand the meaning of a previously hidden thing. It's an "ah ha" moment for you!

Everyone has a gift from God. All the people in your life have one. When our gifts flow in harmony with each other, mankind is healed and restored. This is when miracles occur. People need miracles in their lives that are beyond man-made solutions. That's why God gave you the gift you carry inside.

Do you know your God-given gift? Would you like to know it? I have asked that question hundreds of times to others, and they have all said "yes." The purpose of this book is to help you to discover and then use your gift. Anyone can know their gift and learn how to release it for others.

You were born with a gift from God. That gift inside is waiting to be revealed to you and to the entire world around you. It's why you were born.

Ron Lattier
Raleigh, North Carolina

CHAPTER 1

It's a Gift

I was four years old, and it was Christmas. Life seemed perfect. I remember the smells coming from Mom's kitchen and the holiday tunes that filled our home.

I'll never forget that huge tree in the living room, nestled in the corner away from the fireplace. Each time I passed by it, I took another look to see if the gift I wanted was there yet under the tree. The days came and went, but it was not to be seen.

Mom had known for months the gift I wanted that Christmas. It was the only gift that I had requested. Of course, I had been the perfect child, and I just knew that I would receive my one gift. So I continued to look and to believe for that gift. In time, I did receive my gift. It had been there all the time. Mom had hidden it behind a larger box.

Everyone I know loves receiving a gift. You hope that the gift is one you like and can use. If it comes from Mom or a friend, it usually is of course.

Have you ever had someone actually hand-make a gift for you? Such a gift is an original, one of a kind. When I was a child my grandfather carved a whistle for me from a piece of wood and inscribed my initials on it. He had done other whistles for my cousins, but they looked different from mine.

A heartfelt gift is always an original, and it's like that with God too. God's gift to us is very original and one of a kind because we are one of a kind.

My friend Kelli has always had a special gift from God. Kelli and I grew up together from early childhood. She was the best student in our class, but I was a close second to her. Kelli went on to marry her high school sweetheart, and they are still together after raising four children. Kelli's gift is that she can see into you where the pain, the hurt and the struggles of life occur. Even when we were children, she could tell me in a moment what was wrong with me. Often, Kelli will see a picture in her mind to describe the issue I'm struggling with, and she is always accurate. Her discernment is a gift from God.

Perhaps you have known someone like Kelli. Their gift just flowed from them to others. It was neither a learned attribute nor a developed talent. The gift was spontaneous. Kelli will tell you that she has learned when and how to speak this gift into another person. Some places and moments are just not appropriate, even for such an amazing gift.

We all need people like Kelli to speak into our lives at crucial moments of decision. God gave her this gift to help others. God also wants you to share your gift with the world, to bless, to heal and to help many.

Gifts are not talents. A talent or a skill can be developed; a gift cannot. Did you ever watch a bricklayer? My friend Cliff is working on an entrance to a new planned community of homes. I watched him working on it recently. His skill level was obviously well developed. I had no idea how he could do such a great job, yet Cliff made it appear so simple. I asked him how he had become so good at it.

"Well," he said, "I have been doing this now for thirty years, so it's just natural for me." He had certainly learned how to do it well. Through much practice he had become an expert mason.

All of us have talents or skills which we have become good at doing in life, and the world is better for our contribution, but that's not the same as a gift from God. Your God-given gift was placed inside of you at conception. It cannot be improved beyond what it already is. It is a perfect gift given by a perfect God.

I do believe that we can learn how to release our gift. I cannot tell you the number of times when I have spoken my gift at the wrong moment. A friend of mine often reminds me that truth spoken out of time becomes hurtful, and she is correct.

While our gift is perfect, we are not. We have to learn to recognize the inner voice of God's Spirit directing us in releasing the gift to others. Also, we must learn to observe when the moment is right for our gift to flow. My suggestion is to be kind and gentle to yourself in the learning process. Just let the exercise of your gift become natural for you.

Gifts and talents can complement each other in your life. I'm inclined to think that they should do so. For example, my friend Sandy is a massage therapist. Experiencing one of her hour sessions is simply Heaven on Earth. I go as much as possible and love every moment of it. Sandy is a perfect example of someone merging a Gift of Compassion with healing talents. She just looks at you with genuinely compassionate eyes and a caring heart. Sandy's gift is from God, while her talent has been learned through training and experience.

For patients like me, it is obvious that Sandy allows the gift and the talent to work together in her healing sessions. I find this merger to be common among people. We may not recognize so easily the God-given gift in the mix. Yet, it is always present.

It's a Gift

Do you enjoy attending birthday parties? I love the ones where the host prepares an array of delightful dishes and unique foods. Yes, I love to eat, and I assume that you do too. Of course, we both have maintained that perfect shape we had in high school. Well, I recently attended a birthday party for twins. I arrived a little late, and upon entering saw a large table filled with gifts. I placed my gifts where they would be opened first.

I know the girls we were celebrating that evening well, and they have always been very competitive with each other. Theirs is like a lifetime contest. Everyone has thought this was so unnecessary, since both the girls have been successful in life. After two hours, we were all ready for them to open their gifts, but, for some reason, they never did.

The next week I saw one of the twins in a coffee shop and I asked her about it. As we sat and talked for a while, Ann said to me: "We didn't open our gifts because we felt that one of us might receive a more expensive gift than the other." I could hardly believe what I was hearing. Imagine not opening a gift because of jealousy or pride! Could it be possible that a person might also refuse God's gift to them?

Accepting and releasing the gift that God has placed in you should be a natural experience, much like breathing or eating. You can just do it because it's there.

My gift is never in competition with the gift of another person. The desire is for our gifts to harmonize for the good of someone in need. Life is never just about me, but always about us.

Before we had finished talking, that day, I encouraged Ann to open her gifts at next years' birthday party, and I'll let you know if she does. I told her that if she didn't open my gift to her, I would open it myself. You should have seen the look I received from her! The only problem I have with opening gifts has to do with the required waiting.

Let's be happy for every God-given gift flowing through us. It's life's best feeling to know that you have helped someone. Just be you, and let that gift bless another person. That, in itself, is reward enough. Pray, "God, please use me to help him or her today on their journey with You."

A GIFT FROM GOD IS NEVER EARNED

A gift from God is never earned. I know that's not easy to believe, but it's true. Like you, I was reared to believe that rewards followed acts of work or obedience. Now that's usually true with natural things, but not so with the supernatural, the things of God. God alone decides the gift you receive. Just be happy with your gift.

Remember: God's gift has always been present in your life. Thus, earning it was never an issue. Learning how to release the gift, however, is an ongoing, lifelong pursuit. Focus on knowing and releasing your gift for the good of others.

YOUR GIFT FROM GOD CANNOT BE HIDDEN

Your gift from God cannot be hidden. Sometimes others may see it in you even before you see it in yourself. The people around you are easily drawn to the gift within you.

A good friend, Kari, describes the first time she met Richard: "It was like I felt drawn to this man. Each time I have seen him since that first meeting, there is this intuitive connection I sense with him. It is not a physical attraction, but a spiritual one." Yes, your gift will speak louder to others than your words will.

YOUR GIFT FROM GOD CANNOT BE LOST

Your gift from God cannot be lost. I have a collection of stuff that I call "memory objects." These are little things that special people in my past gave me. For example, my dad gave me an old quarter when I was twelve years old.

We were at the beach on a summer vacation when Dad said to me: "You will soon become a young adult, and life will change for you. My love for you will never change. I will always believe in you. Keep this old quarter as a reminder of my words and of this moment." That quarter is priceless to me. Occasionally I will hold it and revisit my memories of that moment with Dad many years ago. You cannot lose the gift God has placed in your life.

YOUR GIFT FROM GOD CANNOT BE DENIED

Your gift from God cannot be denied. I first met Seme at a conference on recognizing and preventing child abuse. He was a native of Thailand but had moved to America five years earlier. I listened intensely as Seme shared with the conference his story. His three younger sisters had all been sold into child slavery and prostitution. When Seme finished his training as a therapist, he told us, he would return to Bangkok to help those coming out of child prostitution.

The entire audience was in tears, as we listened to Seme that day. God gave Seme the Gift of Mercy. Even in his pain and remorse for his three sisters, Seme could offer mercy to others caught up in the same plight and condition. A gift from God will not be denied, and the gift that God has given you must be shared with others.

YOUR GIFT FROM GOD CANNOT BE SEPARATED

Your gift from God cannot be separated. Each of us has a mind, a body and a spirit.

The gift that God gave to you is woven into all of those parts of you, so that it is impossible to separate the gift from the three parts of your being. When your God-given gift flows to another person, all three parts of your makeup are involved in that moment.

Our spirit perceives a need, and our gift is activated. Then our mind processes it, and our body expresses the gift to the needy person. Of course all this happens almost simultaneously within us. God made you a complete person and placed within you a gift to be given away to all humanity.

YOUR GIFT FROM GOD CANNOT BE DUPLICATED

Your gift from God cannot be duplicated. You are unique and one of a kind. No one on earth is exactly like you. How you perceive life and express your feelings defines your own person and makes you different from all others. While the same gift may be in many people, the expression of it varies with each one. God always positions the right person with the right gift to meet someone's need at just the right moment. So, release your gift and see a need met.

My friend Terry and I often meet on Friday mornings for coffee and a chat. I came to know him several months ago through a mutual friend. Terry is married and has two active young boys.

Terry was in the healthcare industry for more than twenty years. Then, two years ago, he was laid off from his well-paying corporate position. But God never makes mistakes with our lives. Terry has the Gift of Administration with the ability to connect people. Since being laid off, instead of wallowing in self-pity, he has started several new companies and has networked with dozens of other people as partners in business, many of them previously laid off themselves. Isn't that interesting? One gift always complements and connects to other gifts. Bless you, Terry.

Life is more important than just making a lot of money or having a prestigious position. All of that is temporary and is easily lost. Your gift from God is eternal and connects you to others in a divine plan for the well-being of all cultures.

Perhaps you have or will (like Terry) find yourself in a life transition. Don't panic, but look for God's purpose in it. It may be to help you discover that gift inside. When you do find your gift, life will never be as it was before. You'll suddenly know the real reason for which you were born, my friend.

CHAPTER 2

It's Your Best Moment

As Sela stood before her university graduating class, she had a lot to be thankful for. She had been an only child, and her mom had raised her all alone, since her dad had died when she was only three years old. I was blessed to have known both Sela and her mom for many years and to have watched their lives unfold.

Sela's mom longed to see her only daughter graduate from a university, but it was not to be. She was not there that day to see Sela give her commencement address, having died just five months before from a sudden and severe stroke.

As Sela began to speak that day, she said: "Mom, we did this together. I know you are watching from Heaven, and I thank you for believing in me. Mom, I love you and I will make you proud of me." As you can imagine, there was not a dry eye in the audience.

Added to this is the fact that Sela was born without arms and struggled in school because of multiple learning disabilities. Still, both she and her mom were determined that she would graduate from a major university. And now she had done it — with a perfect grade point average.

Now here is the rest of Sela's story: She was given by God the Gift of Leadership. Yes, in spite of her handicaps and disadvantages, the girl was a natural-born leader.

Sometimes I think God has a unique sense of humor because God gives us a gift that no one else recognizes as even being possible. Sela had become the leader for this graduating class of thousands, and she will continue to exercise her leadership gift for a lifetime. I'm delighted that she is my friend. Go, girl!

You can exercise your God-given gift 24/7, and nothing should be allowed to prevent you from doing it. Examples like Sela inspire us all. Sela was always at her best when exercising her Gift of Leadership. I asked her, following the commencement address, "When do you feel that you are at your best moment?"

Sela's quick reply was profound, "When I am flowing in my Gift of Leadership."

Since God made all of us, then God must know how we can best be fulfilled in life. The ideal way to be you is simply to go with the flow of your gift.

THE GIFT WITHIN YOU

Have you ever done something that you just knew you should do, but you were terrified doing it? Well, a few years back I did this. I was living in a different state than my parents when I received the terrible news that Mom had been diagnosed with cancer. She and I had been rather close, but we had also had our moments (you will understand). I was crushed when I received this news about her.

My brother was living beside our parents at the time, and I'm sure this experience was far more difficult for him than for me. Mom went on to live for a few more years after that initial diagnosis, and then she went home to Heaven one Monday morning. I was blessed in that I was there with her when she died.

I know that moment was most horrible for Dad. He had faithfully cared for Mom throughout her illness. There is no one on earth like my dad.

I knew that God wanted me to speak at Mom's funeral. I tried desperately to convince myself that this was not so, but I could not. When I finally told Dad and my brother, they were both fine with it.

I thought and prayed a lot about what to say in such a brief few minutes. I also doubted that I could do it and keep my composure. I wasn't afraid to show my emotions in public, but I did want the audience to understand my remarks.

We finished all the preparations, and the morning of the memorial service arrived. I stood and spoke as if I had been preparing myself for that moment my whole life. The lady who was our representative from the funeral home said at the conclusion of the service: "That was the most amazing presentation at a memorial service I have ever heard." I felt uncharacteristically speechless. My gift had flowed well, and it was my best moment. Thank You, God!

Do you enjoy your career? I am told that most people would prefer another career – if it were possible. Would you? I have an opinion (we all do) why this is so. It's because too many of us do not know what our gift from God is. Once you do, build your career around that gift. If you do, you will be extremely fulfilled and highly successful in it. Later, I will write an entire chapter on a career and your gift.

Do you remember when you were a teenager? Yes, I know it's not been that long ago and, of course, you still look as good as you did then. Well, last Saturday, while I was visiting some friends who live near the beach, I chatted with a sixteen-year-old guy named Jeff.

I had previously chatted with Jeff's parents about him and his God-given gift. He and his dad had just returned from a humanitarian trip to Central America, and while on that trip, this teenage son had become very aware of his unique gift. He had a Gift of Knowledge about the needs of strangers he met, and he used his gift to help the needy to understand their problems and to receive help with them. It was a defining moment in his life.

I chatted with Jeff, as I had with his parents for over an hour to encourage them and to clarify what had occurred. You can learn early in life what your God-given gift is. That trip and what occurred to Jeff was his best moment, and I'm convinced that his gift will positively influence large numbers of people in the future.

Whatever Jeff decides to do as a life career, his gift will drive it to success. Educate yourself well and integrate your gift into it. This will guarantee your success in any career and in any setting of life.

Every living person should meet my dad. He is the most amazing man I have ever known. Yes, I know that he is my dad, but I'm also right about his uniqueness of person and gift. Dad has an awesome Gift of Communication. He has never been without words for others in any situation. People just love being around him to talk and to learn.

I've watched Dad chat both with average persons and highly influential ones, and they all feel identity and comfort with him. Sometimes I think God poured a big bucket of "communication with love" all over Dad. I'm not sure he even realizes how good he is at talking with anyone on any subject.

That's how a God-given gift works in us. People simply cannot resist as you share. It's your best moment.

For example, when I was about twelve one day I went to work with Dad, who was the manager of an aluminum supply company. It was one of those school days when parents took their child with them to their workplace for the day. I had planned this day for weeks. I knew what I would wear (I had to look good, of course), and I knew that Dad would be so very happy to have me with him, to help. I might even be offered a future job with the company – maybe a Vice President's position with a big corner office and a great view of the city. (Well, back to reality.)

Just after lunch (we had Chinese) two men came in the front door to the reception area. Of course, I was watching everything, just in case they needed me to solve some pressing problem (ha! ha!).

Apparently the two men had not received items they had ordered for their business, and they were very upset about it. Their voices became rather loud, and Dad heard them too, so off we went toward a hostile encounter.

For about five minutes Dad just listened to the two men, and then he began to speak to them in a very calm voice.

One of the men said to Dad, "Why, I might just buy this company and become your boss."

Dad smiled and gently replied, "Well, if you do, please allow me to keep my job." With this, we all began to laugh. All of the tension had left the room.

Since Dad was handling the matter, I left to get a cold drink from the soda machine in the back, and on my way I marveled at what I had just witnessed. Dad was so good with those men that I felt in that moment that I really wanted to be like him. Such is the God-given Gift of Communication mixed with kindness and diplomacy.

Didn't you just love that story? And it really did happen just that way.

It's summer as I write this, and I'm loving it. I even have a rather nice tan (that's always been easy for me to get). I like the packs of stretchy, multi-colored wrist bands that you find in the summer in so many stores. Some of them have meaningful words written on them, and they look nice when you wear them. I'm looking at one on my left wrist right now that says, "Best," and that reminds me of my gift as the best part of me that I have to offer to others. Yes, I know it's a simple thing, but, hey, it works for me.

You can never forget about your God-given gift and rely, instead, on your persuasive words and abilities. These are never a good substitute for that gift inside of you that came from God. If it helps you too, go buy a pack of the cool colored summer wrist bands. Of course, you also need to work on that tan at the beach.

Some of us struggle to say "no" to another task or job challenge. Somehow we feel like we must be the best person for the job since we were asked to do it. Of course we may have been the fourth on a list of possible people for it. Nevertheless, we smile politely and say, "Yes." Later we feel just awful for ignoring the family while trying to catch up on all that extra work.

I am sure that many of you have had such moments (not that I have, of course). While it is true that a few people can work well on overload (note the *few,* please), the rest of us just burn out like a distant, dying star in the heavens. I prefer a twinkling star where there is still life.

Is there a point here? Yes, just be you and do those tasks that flow from your gift. Honestly, you don't have more than one primary gift from God? That's why they call it primary, dear. Learn to say "no" to some things, and just do what you are good (the best) at, and the world will love you for it.

Cari is maybe five feet tall in heels, but she is "a girl to be reckoned with," as they say in the South. (Incidentally, you can buy online now a how-to-talk-southern dictionary.) Cari works at a five star restaurant here in the city where I live (most of the time). While I love their food, I also ask to be seated in her area of the restaurant. She is so much fun to watch and to chat with when she bounces by. I'm told Cari makes more on tips than the manager receives as a salary.

What you don't know is that Cari has a PhD in a highly respected discipline and has been recruited by universities all over for a professorship. However, she so loves serving and encouraging all of us over dinner that, so far, no one can convince her to leave the restaurant. Cari has found the best in her Gift of Service and Encouragement in this setting. That she just loves what she does with a passion is obvious. My friend Cari has found her best moment in living out her gift from God.

I have a feeling that some of you reading this are thinking that you wish you could find your best moment of living out your

God-given gift too. Oh, you can. That gift inside of you, which has always been there, is just pleading to come out and live in the world. While most change is not easy, some change is necessary. Life is too brief to just do a job for a paycheck. You were created for more than just surviving. Your gift is a God thing which reflects your purpose for living. Please discover it and allow it to be expressed as the real you.

If necessary, be willing to change careers or to relocate to another city. You deserve to be happy and fulfilled in life with that gift flowing out of you 24/7. Someone is waiting for you and your gift to bless them in their organization or business. When you find that place and fill it with your gift, life will suddenly make sense, and you'll love every single day of it. These are the moments for which you were created.

College internships can be exciting, or they can be rather dull, and most of us were required to do one for graduation. I did mine in sunny Florida, but not on the beach. Oh, yes, I had visions of lying on the beach and being served by several happy, young faces, but I had to come back to reality.

While in Florida for my internship, I worked with a non-profit organization and had a most intriguing supervisor. Garnett was an older man who had seen much of life and survived it all. He was a navy corpsman in World War II, assigned to the Marines in the Pacific. His war stories were enlightening, and his manner in describing them was consuming.

To say that Garnett was a most unique personality would simply not be sufficient. He was one of those persons that you just never forget. Garnett had a Gift of Faith and Persuasion that flowed out of every word he spoke.

Prior to working with that non-profit, Garnett had sold life insurance. I was told (and I do not doubt it) that he was the most successful life insurance salesman the company had in its history. I know that summer Garnett convinced me that I could go to graduate school and become a person of great influence for good. He was a man of unusual faith and persuasion. It was a gift from God. That gift blessed his world and many of us interns.

Please discover your gift from God. The people God has placed in your life need it. None of us have a complete picture of how we affect each other on this journey called life. Your gift may be crucial to someone whom you love. It could be the very thing that they need to move forward into their future.

Too many of us feel that we are not gifted from God, but you are. I know that you are. Once you discover that gift inside of you, your life will shine like the morning sun rising over the sea. I promise you it will. It will become your best moment in life.

When I flow in my God-given gift, I am most happy, fulfilled and productive. It's like winning a gold medal in the Olympics. The amazing reality is that it repeats itself when that gift operates through me for others.

And you were meant to experience the same. Your gift is uniquely expressed through you. So, discover it, enjoy it and bless the world with it.

CHAPTER 3

Discovering Your Gift

Lea sat in my office with tears running down her cheeks and asked: "What am I good at in life?" She was a high school junior and was taking a series of standard tests to help determine her career alternatives. You remember those, I'm certain. Most of us were terrified that we would discover that we were not that good at anything — regardless of our grade point average. Life is still like that for many teens today.

Lea cried, "I feel like they are telling me I'm a failure and have no future." Of course I encouraged her that this was not so. I had watched her grow into young womanhood since she and her family lived on my street. She was a good student, with above average grades, and would certainly be accepted into a university. So what was the problem that led her to my office?

Lea already knew her God-given gift, but she was afraid she could not use it in a career. Dad wanted her to be a professional woman who would make an exceptional salary. Mom wanted grandchildren (soon). So there was Lea caught between two loving parents who had strong opinions about their daughter's future. But what did Lea want? I asked her that question.

"I want to be a nurse, serving in a Third World country, helping people who have no medical care," she said.

Wow! Talk about a goal for life! She had a beautiful picture of hers. Lea had the Gift of Compassion, and people were all that mattered to her.

Discovering your gift from God is easy. Actually we have already seen it in action in our lives. Most of us just did not have a name for it, nor did we understand it. While a few others in our lives saw our gift, they did not know how to help us with it. So it's easy to see why few people know or understand their gift.

How do you discover your gift from God? Well, the first question to ask is: "Do you really want to know what your God-given gift is?" Again, this is not just one of your talents or abilities. Talents and abilities can be improved and developed, but this gift from God within you is always present and already perfect. You just have to discover it and release it.

I'm going to assume that you want to know what your gift is. So let's begin the journey of discovery. Here's what I want you to do:

Find a quiet room where you can ponder your life, and tell everyone that you need some private time. Trust me, they can wait for a while.

Take a notebook and a pen with you and go into that quiet room. Try to clear your mind of work and responsibilities. Relax and think about your life from childhood. As you do this, you should be able to recognize that from childhood and forward a certain gift was very obvious in your life. For example:

- People would come to you for counsel and advice.
- Friends loved being around you since you always encouraged them.

- You just seemed to know what was troubling other people.
- You would pray for others, and they would get better.
- When you spoke, it captivated the audience.
- People just naturally followed you wherever you led them.

Now write in your own words what you remember of these moments. As you follow the trail of your life and your gift, detail it all on paper. If you will do this sincerely, you will see a pattern of your gift developing and flowing out of your life to others. It was a very good moment — for you and for them. And still today, your gift is flowing from you to others.

Kori sat on the front row of the class that I was teaching on gifts. It was a weekend event, and the class was completely full. She came an hour early to get an up-front seat.

It was obvious that the girl was anticipating a life-altering moment during the class. I could see the expectation in her green eyes, as she peered up at me.

I had taught on about a dozen gifts when it happened. As I finished presenting the material on the Gift of Helps/Services, Kori jumped to her feet and shouted, "This is me! This is me!" We all paused and just looked at her with grins of delight.

I had asked the class the week before to do the quiet room exercise mentioned above. Kori did and discovered for herself that she had always flowed in the Gift of Helps/Services. The class provided for her the assurance that she was correct. That's a life-changing moment for anyone.

Give your gift a name. For example:

- Wisdom
- Encouragement
- Discernment

- Healing
- Teaching
- Leadership

This will help you to identify your gift from God. It will also clarify for you why you are so good and natural at doing certain tasks in life. Of course, when you know what your gift is *not* it will free you from the self-criticism of doing tasks well of which you are not gifted. In this way, learning what your God-given gift is will revolutionize your life for the better.

When I discovered that my gift had an identifiable name, it reassured me of its legitimacy. It also helped me to understand all those times as a child when the gift operated in my life.

Some gifts are less understood by others and, thus, are often not accepted. That can confuse a child. I had doubts about my gift because no one around me understood or appreciated the gift within me. Later in life, when I and others near to me accepted with knowledge my gift, everything changed for the better. God actually used my gift to help them, and now I had a name for it. You can know the name of your gift too.

Chat with family and friends about your gift. Don't let your age or other life factors prevent you from talking with them about it. Most of your family and friends want to help you with life. If necessary, just ignore those who do not want to help.

Yes, I know we all have some of them. Listen to the helpful comments from those who have known you and who have been in your life. They will confirm your belief about the gift within you. Remember: they care about you and will usually be honest with you.

This is, most often, a perfect way to affirm the gift that you carry inside. After all, your family and friends have benefited from your gift in actual life experiences. It has always helped them.

Robert had always wanted to be an elementary school teacher. He loved children and had taught classes at his church and community center for kids. His parents told him that he should be an attorney like his dad. After all, attorneys make more money than teachers and are highly esteemed within any community.

Robert had asked his high school counselor, his pastor, his friends and family what they thought about his career choice. They all told him he was a gifted teacher. When I explained to Robert the Gift of Teaching he said, "Yes, I know that's me!" And Robert wisely decided to choose a life career around his gift. Today he is an honored and fulfilled elementary teacher here in the city where I live.

Read some good books on your gift. While there are numerous books available, be discerning and choose those that really speak to your gift and person. Some of the best ones may not be the most expensive to buy. Of course, you can go online to find a wealth of material on your gift.

If you are a person of faith, I encourage you to consult the Bible. It has a wealth of knowledge on gifts. You know yourself. That gift inside which continually comes forth is your God-given gift. Please do not neglect or ignore it for lack of knowledge. That gift is you, and it will reveal itself in your life. So please make the most of it for the sake of others, as well as for your happiness. Enjoy your life and the gift within.

Find an expert on your gift. There are a few of us around who help others to discover and to flow in their God-given gift. I consult with individuals and groups on their gifts rather often.

Sometimes coming together with a group in a discovery environment can be very helpful. It's less costly in a group, plus you can interact with others of like interest and giftedness.

The fact is that we educate our minds to function in society and simply ignore our gifts. Few universities offer any classes on discovering your God-given gift. That's a tragic mistake in any culture, and it makes the false assumption that such a gift is not important. Your gift defines you and influences absolutely everything about your life. Thus, your gift is exceptionally important to your life. Pursue every opportunity to know your gift.

Lynn worked for a large manufacturing company as their chief financial officer. She had held several jobs in the company and was presently responsible for all financial disbursements. Weekly, she and her assistants handled millions of dollars in assets for the company. Then she registered for one of my classes on discovering your gift from God.

The class covered numerous gifts, and Lynn was an eager student. When we taught on her gift (administration), she beamed, as if a light had been turned on inside of her. It was amazing to watch her facial response and to listen to her words of excitement.

Later that afternoon, Lynn was called back to work. There had been a major problem with a vendor which could cost the company millions of dollars in lost revenue. The plant might even have to close for several days. Lynn calmly administrated the solution, using the gift that God had given to her, and the crisis was over within twenty-four hours.

The plant manager asked Lynn how she had solved the problem so quickly. "Why, I just used my God-given gift," was her reply.

His response to her was, "Please continue to use it in all of your work. It has saved us a lot of money and loss of production." Now Lynn uses her gift daily at work.

One of the most profound moments in life comes when you discover your gift. It's like a divine connection of purpose, and you suddenly know why you were born. The lights really do go on inside of you. Please do not let fear or pressure prevent you from discovering your God-given gift. It's just too important to miss.

Too many people just go through a routine of survival. For them, life is to be endured and not to be enjoyed. What a tragedy this is! As your friend, I encourage you to explore and to find that gift inside for which your world awaits.

David is a friend who found his gift last year. He had worked for a government agency for more than twenty years, but he confided to me: "I hate my job, but I have security in it. My wife would kill me if I changed careers."

David and his wife Jenny sat in one of my seminars on discovering your gift. They were intrigued by the concept of a God-given gift. Jenny had never thought of it. David had read a book on it years before but had never processed it into his life. They sat soaking in every word on the subject of gifts.

The second day I taught on their particular gift, and the light inside went on. It was simply amazing to watch them when this happened. They came to me after the seminar had concluded and said: "We both are changing careers within our respective agencies. We want to position ourselves to use our gift in the marketplace." Wow! They did it, and they just love the result.

Again, anyone can discover their gift. When you do, you naturally dream of using it. New doors of opportunity will open for you, and that gift you carry inside. When you can use your gift in a career, life's work will become fun and exciting every day.

You will never know what might have been if you ignore your inner gift. Often I see a person's life dream fulfilled when their gift is discovered. There is a direct connection between your dreams and your gift for life. Remember: it's your gift from God that naturally flows out of you and touches a needy world.

CHAPTER 4

Your Gift and Your Family

I met Cathy at church during a social event. She was a single mom of three and worked at a local department store in one of the area malls. Being a consistent mall shopper myself, I would see her occasionally. (I'm told that all intelligent people visit the mall several times a week just to check for seasonal markdowns. Some of you understand. Others, we hope, will become enlightened.)

Cathy was a very busy lady. She took night classes to earn a college degree, as well as working her forty hours a week. And, in all of this, there was no time off from being a mom, so you get the picture of Cathy's life. She had no idea about her gift.

I did an evening seminar at her church on knowing your God-given gift, and she commented before the class began: "Maybe my gift is being a good mom." Well, no one disagrees that being a good mom is a godly calling. Nevertheless, Cathy was to learn in class later that evening what her gift really was.

The college courses Cathy was taking were to become a nurse. But everyone loved it when she served in the church nursery and preschool classes. She had such a healing and comforting touch. It was as if she was Mom to all the kids.

It would have been easy to see Cathy as an awesome nurse, but during our class break, I heard that Cathy was dropping out of nursing classes. She was feeling weary, unsure and out of money. We encouraged her, and the class resumed.

When we taught on the Gift of Healing, Cathy began to weep. She could not control her emotions, as she realized that this was her gift from God. (I'm sure she also must have felt confused about what to do with those nursing classes.)

The following week several businessmen in Cathy's church heard about her plight and decided to help her. A fund was established to assist single moms who wanted to return to school. We all wanted Cathy to use her gift for good and to help heal hurting people. (You can go get your box of tissues now.)

Cathy continued her college classes and graduated as a Registered Nurse. She now serves our city in the Emergency Room of one of the larger hospitals, and everybody just loves her at work. The human family is blessed when you know and use your gift.

Cathy and her three daughters just moved into their new house, and life could not be any better for them. The girls are happy because Mom is happy. Your gift will always bless your immediate family.

Also I believe that love for your family will inspire you to discover your gift and how to apply it in a career. When you do, all the families in your world of influence will be blessed.

Sometimes family communication can be challenging. Would you agree? I thought you would. Too often we simply do not know how to communicate with one another. Men and women have different styles of communication. Individually, we assume that others hear the same information we do, but that's a mistake. It's rare that any two persons comprehend the same data in the same way because we are all different. Thus, it's no surprise that we communicate poorly within our families.

What's this have to do with one's gift? Well, your gift is an extension of God and is intended to unite people. It has the capacity to touch the heart of people, not just their brain. Perception is as much felt as it is processed. Our perception of anything is, for that moment, our reality of it. The gift you carry will unite and bring harmony into the home. Family life is enhanced when we flow in the same direction with each other.

Ginger and Kari are twin sisters who were raised by an aunt after their parents died in a car accident. They both went to the same local university and shared an apartment. The girls related well to each other, but they never considered working together. After graduation, each worked at different careers, yet neither seemed very happy with her work.

When these sisters came to me for advice and counsel, I asked them what they really wanted to do with their lives. We discussed gifts and their particular gift. Neither Ginger nor Kari had ever considered that they each possessed a God-given gift. So we helped them to discover what their particular gift was. You should have seen the smiles and the hugs, when they eventually realized what their gift was. Now they could build a career around that gift.

Ginger was a natural leader, obviously possessing the Gift of Leadership. Kari loved helping and serving others, and so she was gifted with Service/Helps. Together the two of them formed a company that provided care and assistance to business executives and their families. Their business has expanded, is very successful and now employs over one hundred persons.

Siblings who use their God-given gifts together can be extremely successful, so this can work for you as well. Your family is one of life's treasures. Most all of us love and appreciate our family, and therefore, it is normal that we want to bless them.

Being good to your family is being good to yourself. Do you remember those moments growing up when a person outside of your family hurt your brother or sister? You immediately came to the aid of that sibling, even if the two of you were not all that close.

One family I know found very creative ways to help out when their dad was injured and out of work. The whole family pulled together in their moments of need.

Your family needs your gift. God gives families the perfect gift mix for them to be healthy and happy. Each person has a different gift, which will harmonize with the other gifts in the home. God designed that gift with purpose and for your family's well-being. Love becomes your motivating incentive to discover your gift and to make it available for your loved ones. Please do so — for all of them.

Gifts are expressed in unique ways. Daniel was the class clown. He just made everyone laugh. In high school, students would occasionally make fun of Daniel and his carefree spirit. Even the teachers felt that he should be more serious about life. No one realized that this was an expression of Daniel's gift from God.

Daniel's Pastor asked him, "What do you think God wants you to do with your gift?" I'm told that Daniel asked, "What gift?" He did not know humor was a gift. I suppose he just assumed it was how he saw and described the world.

Today Daniel is a hospital chaplain, affectionately called the "Chaplain of Humor." A few caring people in Daniel's life helped him to see how he could use his gift to bless the human family. Trust me: Chaplain Daniel does that very well.

I'm convinced that Daniel also has the Gift of Encouragement. It is expressed beautifully through humor for those who desperately need it. All his patients are so glad he uses it to help them. Life is more than just black and white, so color your world for good with that gift inside of you from God.

How do you use your gift in life? Sometimes I imagine my world of friends and family, with everyone flowing in their gift. I can envision the amazing effects this would have on me and on them. None of us would be hurting, needy or feeling worthless. All of us would be pouring our gift into each other. I love that picture.

"I'm not good enough for God to give me a gift," Rena said. She was an accomplished woman with a professional career, and she had everything: a beautiful home, a loving husband and two adorable children, a corner office overlooking the city skyline, wonderful friends, and three huge closets full of designer clothes. When she made that statement, I looked at her with shock and surprise. How could she not know?

Rena was the oldest of six siblings, and when her Mom died early in life, leaving her to be the necessary substitute mother of the family, she had done it with reluctance.

It was a big job. Their dad worked seven days a week and was never home, so Rena had to be everything for the rest of the family. Still, she had never thought of herself as special or of having a special gift from God.

Now in her late forties, Rena had the time to consider her life. Her children were married, and she began to ponder about who she really was.

When I asked Rena, "What do you want to do with your life? What's your God-given gift?" she had no idea how to answer those questions. Unfortunately, many people do not have an answer. I said to her, "Go home and think about your answers. Then come back to see me in a week." She did that, even telling her husband Jim about it. I knew because he called me the next day to discuss his wife's situation.

A week later Rena came in for an hour session as scheduled. She looked different. As she sat down, I asked her, "So, tell me: what's different about you?"

"I know what my gift is," she shouted. Rena never shouts, so this was a notable moment for her. "I'm a teacher," she cried, with tears flowing. We both reached for a tissue.

Rena handed me a letter from Jim, which simply agreed with her revelation. It was easy to see how she had built a very successful marketing company. She had taught hundreds of people how to do their job and do it well.

"And what's next, girl," I asked.

"I'm going to teach marketing at the university and in seminars around the country," Rena said. She had the Gift of Teaching, and so teaching was natural for her.

Rena had always felt unworthy because of the difficulties of her childhood and her lack of parental encouragement. She was obviously successful, but she had not been personally fulfilled. She had been born to teach and to use her gift from God.

You deserve to know your gift. Discover it for yourself, as well as for your family. Life is too short just to go through the motions, and money is not an end in itself. Fulfillment and value are far more important. When life is finished, you will want to be happy with yourself.

My dad is a very compassionate man. For him, it is a gift from God. When I was a child, I saw his gift demonstrated countless times. I am very aware that his Gift of Compassion has, over the years, influenced me both personally and professionally. I watched him care for my mom, as well as for my step-mom, as they both died with cancer. He was constant and loving, while never complaining about his situation, so it's easy for me to admire and to love him.

When I was about ten, Dad volunteered to teach a church Sunday school class and was given the unenviable chore of teaching a group of unruly teenage boys. They were impossible and everyone seemed to know it but Dad. The rumor was that no one else in the church would teach this particular bunch.

I can only imagine what that class was like. I was in a more civil class down the hall. Suffice it to say that our class felt compelled to pray for Dad every Sunday morning.

Dad was compassionate for those troubled boys, and he remained their teacher for many years. To this day, I am not sure how he survived the experience. I often wondered if their parents had any clue about their little darlings. It seemed to me, back then, that this group would surely eventually become prisoners on some chain gang. They were just that bad, but Dad loved them with a God-given compassion.

What happened to them? Today these boys are medical doctors, lawyers, teachers and successful businessmen, and many of them remain in contact with Dad. Recently, in a setting at that same church, several of them told me how influential Dad had been in their teen years. They still honor him for his years of loving them. Dad is ninety now, but he is still a compassionate servant of God. He has used his gift well.

I have, for years now, allowed that same gift to flow through my life. Sometimes I enjoyed it and, at other times, it was more challenging. But I could always remember my dad and his unfailing example of compassion for others. Your gift from God may be transferred to you from another. It's not a genetic issue, but more of a spiritual one. I suggest that we all embrace our gift and use it always for the good of humanity and the broader family of mankind.

CHAPTER 5

Your Gift and Your Career

Since childhood, Jonathan had dreamed about owning a restaurant. He worked part time in a local grill while in high school, loved it and became even more passionate to own his eating establishment.

Dad convinced Jonathan to attend the university and earn a degree. While he was studying, he and Carl (another student and close friend) opened a fast food place on campus. It was an amazing success. They had to hire part-time help to accommodate their growing clientele. Life was good, and Jonathan was happy.

After graduation, Jonathan looked for an opportunity to buy an existing restaurant. Carl had moved away, so it was just him. When the Italian Villa became available downtown, he was able to secure a bank loan to purchase it. The business had a long history of success, but the previous owners had retired. So the buy looked like a good one for Jonathan.

After a year of struggle and loss, Jonathan came to see me. "What am I doing wrong?" he asked. "I expanded our seating and updated the dinner room, but business is still very slow."

"What about your gift and that of your employees," I asked. He just stared at me with a blank look on his face.

I suggested that we meet his staff and match their gifts with their position at the restaurant. Jonathan was desperate, so he agreed. Sometimes desperation will produce positive change in us.

As it turned out, Jonathan had the Gift of Compassion, but he had allowed his gift to motivate him to hire and place into position the wrong personnel. No one was flowing in their God-given gift, and every employee was miserable in their assigned job. It was no surprise that business was horrible and the morale was so low. Things would have to change quickly if the restaurant was to survive.

It is possible for your gift (like Jonathan's) to be misused. We need a balance from other gifts flowing around us. Unfortunately, Jonathan did not have this at his place of work.

Now everyone was matched by their gift to a position, and within three months the situation had improved, and the restaurant began making a profit. Morale was high at work now as the employees enjoyed their work.

Obviously, Jonathan was delighted. He invited me to come in for a free dinner, and I couldn't help but notice that the place was very busy.

Jonathan and I continue to be good friends to this day. Within a year of having put in place these new policies, the restaurant was experiencing historical growth and profit. The changes made had been simple, but the results had been profound.

It is a wise business owner who places employees in a position based on their gift. Unfortunately few companies consider a person's gift in the hiring process. They just find someone to place in an opening and hope they will be successful. It's no surprise that most companies have such a high employee turnover rate. This could be avoided in any company and would save a large amount of lost revenue and lost production. I believe that within one year any business could see a notable increase in profit if their employees are matched to a position by their God-given gift. In fact, I am certain of it.

Many companies do try to match a person's education and learned abilities to a position. While that process is beneficial, it's not enough to guarantee a successful relationship between employer and employee. A person's gift from God affects everything about them, from perception to application. It's the hidden element that proves to be the key to success in one's work life.

Billy loved helping his dad fix broken things around the house. If you own a home, you know that there is always something in need of repair, and it's normal for a firstborn child such as Billy to follow Dad around and want to help him. For years

Billy and Dad tolerated each other during those repair moments. The reason was that Billy had no idea how to fix anything and couldn't remember which tool was best for which job. He was very out of place in this role, but neither of them knew how to correct the situation. It was bad, really bad!

Sometimes we tolerate a work situation because we don't know what the solution might be. The result is that everyone is frustrated, and the work is not satisfactorily completed. Often this ends with an employee termination and a loss for the company. When this happens, everybody loses.

Tragically what happened with Billy and his dad can become a lifelong pattern that is repeated over and over, and too often we just assume that this is the way their life is to be. But it doesn't have to be that way at all. When Billy had become a young man,

I helped him to discover his gift from God. Today he is happy and fulfilled as an accountant — not a fix-it man.

Are you happy in your career? In one of my recent classes on Discovering Your Gift, I asked everyone present that question, and 89% of the students said, "No." I was not surprised by this large percent of them being dissatisfied.

I followed up by asking, "Do you know what your gift from God is?" No one else in the room was certain of what their gift was.

There is always a relationship between career satisfaction and knowing which gift God has given to you. I have met only a few people who told me they were contented with their career without knowing their gift. Of course, one can be contented without being happy and fulfilled. I prefer the happy and fulfillment side of career life. How about you, my friend? Let's enjoy our work and our life.

Following her dad's funeral, Kathy told me the sad story of his career. He had been a workaholic and felt that working seven days a week was his calling. Being a good provider for the family meant one thing to him. He had to work all the time. So, unfortunately, Kathy had only known him as the man of the house who was never at home. Oh she had loved him, but she never really knew him as a father. Tragically, his career had been his god. I'm certain that he never knew his God-given gift.

"I always wondered who my dad was," she cried. "Because I was an only child, Mom and I did everything together. We shopped, attended church and school events and had dinner alone."

I struggled to maintain my composure and not weep in front of Kathy. Her father was gone now, and it was too late for the two of them to connect as father and daughter. How about you? As long as we are alive, it's never too late in life to discover our gift from God. Please don't wait until your later years. Those whom you love dearly will be forever affected by your decision. That gift was given to you to bless your loved ones, and it can only be given to your family by you. You are one of a kind.

Stephen worked in the Norfolk shipyards for thirty years. He and his wife Betty had no children. They had a deep desire to help Third World cultures. For years they had taken their vacations and traveled to every Third World nation on the planet, and I'm told that they took thousands of dollars in provisions for the people they ministered to on those trips.

Stephen and Betty had the Gift of Giving. They literally gave themselves as well as thousands of needy items. Often Stephen thought of leaving his career so they could actually live in a Third World nation, but they chose not to. "It's our career that provides the means for our giving," they would say. Stephen and Betty are now in Heaven, but their influence lives on eternally. Just ask the thousands whose lives they touched through their giving.

Your career can be and should be an open door through which your gift flows to the world. I'm amazed at the innumerable ways God uses our gift to bless humanity. Let God use you and that gift to touch your world.

"Will I have to change careers, once I know my gift?" some ask. The answer is usually: "Not unless you choose to do so." The more probable solution will be to shift into a position in your company in which that gift can flow and bless the business.

Most managers and bosses prefer you in a position in which you can be effective. They are normally not opposed to you explaining why you feel that a different position would allow you to be more productive for the company. Just explain to them your new knowledge about your God-given gift. If they are reasonably receptive, they will listen. Your enthusiasm will sell them. Within six to twelve months, the transition into your new role will prove itself to be wise and proper. You could be a trend setter for the company. Your willingness to do this will have a long-term positive influence on both you and your employer.

Let me include a brief word to employers: Please be wise enough to include a gift test or evaluation in your hiring and your ongoing education of employees. This will assist you in the proper placement of every person within your company. Plus, this will eliminate most of your employee turnover due to poor performance or job dissatisfaction. After all, the goal is always to make your business more profitable. This approach will guarantee those desired results.

Different cultures embrace career and work from varied perspectives. In the West, we tend to see life revolving around what we do for a living. It's as if we are driven from childhood to prepare for that golden career that will make us wealthy. Thus, our success is dependent upon a career choice. When you sit and ponder such a philosophy of life, it begins to seem rather narrow and shallow. Yes, I do understand the necessity of a good job. It does require income to live. My point is simply that your life is far more than just what you do for forty hours every week as a career. That gift inside of you is very broad and diverse in its applications. Please do not limit it to your career. Let the gift define you 24/7, at work and at play. It was intended to fulfill you as a human being.

Your gift will elevate your career. Most of us enjoy career promotions and the benefits that follow. Perhaps you will receive that breathtaking corner office on the fortieth floor with a prestigious title to match it. Of course, your family would be so proud of you, and the honors would just flow your way. As a people expert, I know that men place a high priority on career success. Yes, I know that some women do as well. But with all of us, your gift is the key to success in life.

You will grow in understanding and in using your gift. The Gift of Wisdom is a perfect example. Shelly had worked with her dad in his auto repair shop since her high school days. She and I attended high school together and were good friends. Shelly was the heart of the business, and everyone just loved her enthusiasm for life. But Shelly's dad was caught in a time warp in his business practices. He thought computers were evil and unnecessary.

Shelly was progressive and suggested to her dad that they update the business. She went to work on him with some revolutionary ideas. After all, she was his little girl, so she could get away with it.

Dad finally gave in to her. He said, "Okay, I'll try your ideas for six months."

Shelly used her Gift of Wisdom, along with some natural upgrades, to improve the operation of the shop, and within three months profits were up 38% and inventory levels were being constantly monitored by a computer. Dad was amazed and decided that he could take a vacation, and Shelly was the new boss in his absence.

Your gift is always active. It has the potential to change for the better whatever you do. When Shelly applied her Gift of Wisdom to that business, everything improved. Today that family owns three auto repair shops with revenues beyond what Dad could have imagined and all because Shelly used her gift in business, and God honored it. After all, God had placed that gift inside of her.

Your gift will promote you when you use it. It doesn't matter what career you have chosen in life. That gift is functional for the corporate executive or the small business owner. The only requirement is for you to allow it to operate in your life and in your career.

I suggest to companies that they try this gift approach for their business for a year and monitor the result. They will prove themselves to be beneficial, and the results will speak loudly for themselves.

Your gift from God is always people focused. Whether you sit at a desk looking at a screen and analyzing numbers all day or lead a corporation as the CEO, you are about people. Gifts were given with people in mind.

Please do not feel that your gift is less valuable than the gift of another. Like the human body, every part is necessary for the well-being of the whole. Simply said, we need your gift to function for all of us. Your gift is crucial for someone who is near to you. That's why God gave it to you and why He placed you in their lives. So bless them with your gift.

David and I grew up together. He was always a nice person whom everyone enjoyed having as a friend. When he was sixteen David fell in love with Susan. I knew her too, and I and many others sensed that Susan was going to hurt David. She had a track record of breaking hearts.

After David and Susan had dated for a year, she suddenly dropped him for no good reason. Suddenly David went from being an A student to being a D student in a matter of weeks. He wasn't sleeping well and he had no appetite, and he looked absolutely terrible. We all tried to help him, but David was so devastated by what Susan had done that it seemed hopeless. Some of us were worried that David might do something drastic. He was acting strange and keeping to himself.

Fortunately, David had a teacher named Fred. Like my dad, Fred was a church class teacher for teen boys, and he was one of those men who just oozed with compassion. Everyone loved Fred and found him to be a caring man.

There was a restaurant near the high school where we all hung out after Friday evening games. (Every town has at least one of them; just ask the kids.) Adults never came into that restaurant on Friday nights. I assume it was our music and chat that kept them away. But this particular Friday night in October Fred came into what we considered to be "our restaurant" and sat down near David. We all saw it and wondered what was up.

Fred and David talked for a while, and then Fred left. David left a few minutes later. We were dying to know what they had said to each other, but no one dared ask David. Interestingly enough, David got better and actually returned to his old self within a few weeks. I never stopped wondering what had happened that Friday night between David and Fred.

Years later I saw Fred after a funeral and asked him: "What did you and David talk about that Friday night in high school that so changed his life?"

Fred just smiled and said, "I told him that I loved him as a student and that he had his whole life ahead of him. 'Do not hurt yourself over her,' I told him, 'but forgive her and let it go.' "

Wow! That was exactly what David needed to hear. Today David is married and has three children and is a successful attorney. Fred used his Gift of Compassion as a teacher to touch a teen named David, and that gift changed David forever.

You carry a gift inside too. You may feel that it lies dormant and wonder if it really matters to anyone. Yes, it does matter to someone. Someone like David is desperate for it. We may never know in this life the impact a gift has had on another. I believe Fred did not know for years about the results of his comments to David. A gift is what you give away to another person. What they do with it may remain a mystery for a season, but eventually it will come to light.

CHAPTER 6

Your Gift Has Seasons

My favorite season of the year is autumn. Perhaps it's because I have such fond memories of the autumns of childhood. I love living where one has an obvious seasonal change. The differences between seasons can be profound. Sometimes it's like going from one season to another in just one day (calendar dates excluded).

One day a friend of mine described to me her gift as "seasonal." I asked her what that meant.

"My gift from God has seasonal emphasis," Jenna said.

This was a rather new approach to gift usage, so I wanted to know more. "Tell me more, please," I pleaded.

"Well, for a season my gift seems to be so active that I cannot quiet it for a moment. Everywhere I go the gift flows from me to everyone – friend and stranger alike. Then suddenly the gift seems to go underground and only comes out occasionally. I'm not sure why this is, but I assume that it's for some reason," Jenna declared.

Others are telling me something similar about their gift. While your gift is always present in you, it may have seasons of activity that are distinct and different. What's been your experience with your gift?

I must confess that this seasonal thing has been my gift experience too. Since I use frequently the gift within me, I am always checking on its status, and there seems to be a mysterious relationship in all of us between our God-given gift and us learning to release it. I find, for myself, that sometimes there are understandable factors as to why the gift seems quiet within and sometimes not.

Obviously, gift usage is activated by a need in those around you, so a personal season of solitude may relax that gift in you. We all need times of rest, so don't let it concern you that the gift is at rest too. Trust me, there will always be a need for your gift. People will draw it out of you. And I'm sure you delight in sharing that gift with them.

THE SPRING SEASON

Your gift will experience a spring-like season. This is a time of birth or of new life coming forth. Embrace this season even though it may be painful because something new is being birthed in you. Your spring season may be the initial revelation of your gift and/or your inner knowledge of it.

This may all be somewhat confusing for you. This is partly due to our general lack of knowledge concerning God-given gifts. Unfortunately very few institutions teach on this subject, so how are we to know much about an inner gift from God? My passion is to help people become aware of their gift and then how to operate in it for the good of mankind. One's life changes drastically for the better when you uncover that gift inside.

It is important, in this season, to remember that your gift is perfect and yet different from abilities or talents. You do not improve on your gift. You do learn how to release it and how to comprehend its usage to others.

Give yourself lots of grace during the spring season. It may seem like being a young child again and having to learn everything about life and people. During this period, you will need to find some trustworthy and experienced advisors in gift usage. They will help you to learn and to grow in your gift. Take the time to find these important persons as you really do need gifted advisors, especially during this spring season.

Please do not rush through this season. The natural tendency is to hurry the process, especially if you tend to be impatient. Of course you and I have never had this problem of impatience, have we? Let the spring season be one of grace and growth, mellowed with a childlike awe and wonder. Just enjoy the moment.

Look for signs of growth during the spring season. You will identify your gift and then watch it flow from you. It will excite and intrigue you. Your life will begin to revolve around the gift inside. Your understanding of the merging of the gift with your natural talents will become more evident too.

Be cautious not to call them both by the same name. They are different, yet complimentary to each other. Most people can describe their learned abilities and natural talents. They just assume that this is their God-given gift. It is not. Even in this elementary season, you will see on occasion your "perfect gift" coming forth to touch others. It's a beautiful moment. You may not fully understand what's occurring, but that gift is present to help another in need. Your gift is meant to be given in all seasons.

Even as a child, Dennis loved helping others, as his mom recalls: "Dennis was a loving child, always looking for ways to help someone. He volunteered to help other students in elementary school. He led school drives to raise funds for families who had experienced loss in the community. He encouraged his third grade class to raise $10,000 for a well in an African village, to provide clean drinking water. He just loved helping others."

The Gift of Helps was evident in Dennis' life, and he grew in his knowledge of that gift from the earliest seasons. Today he works with several non-profits, raising funds to help the needy worldwide. Enjoy the spring season, that time of your journey of gift exploration.

THE SUMMER SEASON

There is another season with your gift that I will call the summer season. Yes, I know that summer follows spring. It's the season in which you find your gift flowing out almost everywhere you happen to be. Now that you have a functional knowledge of the gift, it is natural for it to take on expression in the marketplace. Strangers seem to quickly warm up to you and to that gift you carry, and it feels new and good to you, like a sunny June day.

Now that you see the working of your gift in action and how well others respond to it, you may think for the first time: "This gift in me is real and good." You feel validated and accepted along with your gift.

Your summer season is when you really accept your gift. During the spring season you had moments of comparing yourself with others and of doubt about the validity of your gift. Now you are settled with it and actually like it. After all, God would never give you a gift that you did not enjoy and find fulfillment in.

The more you are comfortable with the gift you have been given, the easier it is for others to become comfortable with it too. Ginger, a friend of mine, says, "Once I fell in love with my gift, others just seemed to follow." I think she's correct.

The gift you have is God's best gift to you. Remember that God made you for that gift, and everything around you and in you God uses to enhance your gift. You know it just couldn't be any better.

The summer season is when you are out and about with your gift. It's not hidden inside anymore, but it is bursting to be seen. My friend Janice describes it in terms of giving birth to her first son: "I had his name chosen and was more than ready for him to come out." All you moms will understand her words.

This season is when you realize that the gift in you is not just you but is a reflection of God through you. Honestly now, none of us are that good. People may try to elevate you as a result of your gift. Please do not allow yourself to be caught up in the moment. Just remember that you are a servant called to give to others a gift to help them in life's journey. It's never really about you, but about them.

The summer season is when your gift begins to be acknowledged. You have known about the gift in you for years, but few others have. Now, suddenly, many people know about your gift. They identify you by that gift you carry 24/7. This can become a little intimidating, since you may feel that others love the gift more than they do you. Go easy on them, for they are admiring what God has given to you. After all, it was given to you for their sake, right? Just stay focused on who you are, and everything will be fine. Accept the fact that once people see your gift, they are not likely to forget it.

Some gifts are acknowledged more than others. For example, a Gift of Healing may be more prominent than a Gift of Patience. People are drawn to any gift that meets their need at the moment. They acknowledge it in appreciation, and life continues. Just be yourself and feel grateful that God used your gift to help that person. All gifts are equally important.

The summer season is when your gift begins to merge with your talents. Often the two will unite to form a rather unique expression of care and love for the needy. God does not intend for your perfect gift to compete with your developed talent. Instead, they will blend together and complement each other in a most beautiful manner. Think of your own gift and how wonderfully it unites with your natural talents. Only God could orchestrate such a lovely combination. Your talents are developed around your interests and desires in life. The gift you carry will always flow in harmony with your talents. It's a beautiful thing to see.

Emily is a very crafty and contemplative girl. She has her chatty moments but really enjoys the quiet and the creative. She carries the Gift of Creativity. Emily is in the season of summer with her gift. She is very good at expressing it, and it draws everyone to her. It's as if she sees something and then creates it in a visual. We all enjoy her gift and the amazing beauty that's revealed through her as a result. Emily influences hundreds of people each week with her creative gift and her learned talent of expression. I pray that she never stops giving to others.

THE AUTUMN SEASON

Autumn is the most special season of all for your gift. You now have accumulated both knowledge and experience with the gift God has given to you. You almost feel as if you have arrived with it. Even those around you sense the same maturing in you and also in the gift within.

The feeling you have about your gift is magnificent. Finally there is the realization that you can flow in it anytime. You know that you are available 24/7 to help others with the gift you carry. There is a satisfaction in the gift that is beyond words. Life is different now and so fulfilling. People seek you out for help, and your gift precedes you in life.

Lisa has prophetic insight and can provide a clear word for an uncertain situation. I have watched the girl share her gift with others, and it's amazing to see how helpful that gift is to them. People pursue her for help in making the correct decision in matters of life and family, for God has graced her with such insight, and she is living in her autumn season of giftedness. Thank you, girl.

Autumn is when that gift matures. It now seems to flow so easily to others at their moment of need. You realize how much they need what God has placed inside of you, and now it's clear that the gift was always intended to relieve suffering and to eliminate confusion. Maturity brings a new level of awareness that your gift is important, but no more so than the gift in others. You feel a release from having to perform for anyone. It's so natural now to simply be you.

Autumn is when your gift is more focused. You are so content with your gift that you don't always think about it. It's just there, and you know it. Life is good, whether you are flowing in the gift or not. Nevertheless, the gift you carry can, in a moment's time, pinpoint a need and provide the necessary answer. It requires no pre-thought or preparation. The gift just hits the target of the issue.

People are awed, but you can keep it all in balance. It's just a God-given gift. You are as human as any other person. You occasionally need the gift of another. Finally you can relax, feel focused and just be you with that gift.

Autumn is when you wait to release your gift. People are complex, and it's always appropriate to listen to them for the complete story. Most human needs are intertwined with many issues. Releasing your gift into someone prematurely can be a mistake. You have learned to wait and to listen for the details and the proper timing to share that gift. In this way, nothing is left to assumption, and your gift immediately produces positive results.

Thomas, an exceptionally caring and patient person, is a high school science teacher. He and I have served together on committees, and I am always amazed by his Gift of Knowledge at work in any given situation. He just sits and listens and forms a picture in his mind of the problem. Then he suddenly describes the issue in detail and tells us all the perfect solution.

The startling truth is that Thomas is always correct. I caught his wife shopping at the mall one day and asked her, "Is Thomas like this at home, too?"

She looked at me with a little grin and said, "Yes, that's my Mr. Patience. I told him to bottle the gift and sell it so I could retire from work!" Don't you just love a wife's honesty about her husband?

Autumn is when you are comfortable in sharing with the gifts of others. I watched my friend Elle and two other ladies chat with a homeless couple in the parking lot one day. All three of the ladies united their gifts to help that needy couple. All three ladies were very comfortable in sharing together their gifts for the good of the needy, so that the homeless couple received more than they had requested.

This is a beautiful approach to reaching those in crisis. The ladies were focused on the hurting ones. Releasing your gifts as a team enhances their effectiveness. It's easier to share as a team if you do not have ego issues.

Autumn is when you can easily receive another's gift into your life. You have learned an equal respect for all gifts. Those who carry gifts different from yours are now highly appreciated. You see clearly your need for receiving their gifts, and it is a joy to do so.

It's equally pleasurable to give or to receive a gift. If you are in a situation in which another person has the same gift that you carry, and a needy person is present, it's okay for the other person to share their gift with the needy. You are comfortable sharing or not.

Autumn is when you recognize a moment in which it is not proper to share your gift. Some may resist the sharing of your gift with them. That's their decision. I suggest respecting their choice. Their resistance may be due to pride, to fear or to not understanding about God-given gifts. Don't be offended by it.

Toni has the Gift of Faith, and she does not accept "no" as a final answer when it comes to helping someone. Recently, however, I watched her attempting to help a lady who was ill. They were new neighbors, the sick woman was elderly, and she apparently had no friends or family to assist her. So Toni was coming to her rescue.

After Toni had made numerous attempts to be a guardian angel, the woman finally told her, "Please, just leave me alone. I prefer being sick. People give me attention and sympathy that I never had when I was well." Wow! It can happen. Accept the fact that occasionally you may be told "no," but keep sharing that gift with the 98% who will appreciate receiving it.

THE WINTER SEASON

The winter season of your gift may be the most rewarding season of all. You have touched thousands of lives with your gift. You could even write a book or two detailing your experiences. The memories are numerous, and most of them are joyful. Those you have touched will always remember. They are such a precious part of your life because of the God-given gift and your willingness to share it. Life has been good, and you feel validated.

The winter season of your gift circles into completeness. You have seen the enduring results of your gift in the lives of others. Many people have remembered to thank you over the years. You carry inside a feeling of wholeness and of purpose fulfilled. This is simply beyond human words to describe. Life feels good and so worthwhile. Sometimes you feel as if you can see God smiling over your life. Life is not concluded, just understood in light of the gift.

Not long ago, late one night I received an email concerning the death of a dear friend. Ronald had served several generations faithfully with his gift. He could draw together the hearts of every age in any setting. I watched his unique Gift of Communication and Leadership at work. People just loved following him.

Ronald knew all of us by our first name, and his personal care for everyone was unmatched. Now there was an eternal completeness for Ronald and the gift of God he had carried.

The winter season of your gift is when you become a mentor. Yes, you have become that good at sharing your gift, so there is in you now a heartfelt desire to help others with their gift flow. In fact, it has become something of a driving passion. People have actually been pursuing you to mentor them because you're now a living expert at what you do. And you now find watching others learn how to flow in their gift very rewarding and enjoyable.

Art is a retired postal worker whose love for people is as big as the moon. He has the Gift of Visual Creation. What does that mean? He can visualize a thought or a feeling and will find a real-life scene reflecting his mental image and take a picture of it. This is such an amazing gift, and I have seen the effects of his creative pictures on those who are suffering. It provides a relief and a healing for many of them.

Art's passion now is to train others to do the same thing. He tells me, "I love seeing new friends accept this same gift in them. They light up when they realize that God can use them in the same way. It's as if I am living my life a second time through these students." Art is an awesome mentor.

The winter season is when you give more than you receive. It seems that you have an audience everywhere you go. People just want to hang out with you. You do not mind this. It actually feels very good that so many care so much about you.

Life has not stopped. It has just taken a different curve of the road. Now people think that if they are near you your gift will rub off on them. Of course it's not that simple, but you are delighted to give them your attention and the benefit of your gift without any cost.

I'm reminded of my dear friend Bridget. She has the most incredible Gift of Hospitality anyone could possess. Every time I visit her I feel overwhelmed with her care and consideration. It's simply amazing to see. And the girl can cook like a five-star chef. I've told her often that she should open a restaurant or develop a cooking show for television.

Lately I have noticed how Bridget gives away to younger women her secrets of hospitality, and they soak her words up like a sponge does water. She is the most gifted person with hospitality I have ever met, and she loves sharing her gift. Thank you, Bridget, for blessing us all.

The winter season of your gift can be a time of new beginnings. Does that surprise you? I know that a winter season can seem lifeless, but it does not have to be. All winter days are not cloudy. The winter season of your gift can be a rebirth of it.

Remember that your natural age has little to do with your gift. That gift is active and waiting to be engaged. Its usage is really dependent upon you and your posture of heart and mind. So live to share that gift with the world. Life is never over until you have stopped living it.

THE SEASONS OVERLAP

The seasons of your gift overlap. Sometimes it seems as if you are jumping from one season to another and then back again. Please do not let this concern you, for it is normal. The flow and the life of your gift are spontaneous, and so it is with the seasonal movements of that gift too.

God will direct the gift in your life as it is needed by others. Just remember: it's really God's gift inside of you.

The seasons of your gift do not necessarily coincide with your age. They vary with every unique individual. Just be you and enjoy God's gift.

The attitude of your life affects the seasons of your gift. Mr. Lea was a caretaker of an old mill near my parents' home, and I have fond memories of visiting with him as a child. His life must have been rather simple but peaceful.

Mr. Lea was a kind and gentle man with a big smile and a love for life that you could feel. I can almost see him now welcoming Mom and me, after we had walked down to the mill for a Saturday afternoon visit. I saw his loving attitude and genuine care for me. Oh, I know he was like that with everyone else too. He made me want to love and to enjoy life as God had meant it to be.

I am fortunate to have known Mr. Lea. His Gift of Joy has affected me to the present. Our life attitude definitely does influence our gift and its influence on others.

In whatever season of your gift you are living, please enjoy it. When you do, others will enjoy it too. I'm reminded of Jason, a dear man who pastors a church. He deeply loves every person who attends his services. Jason carries in him the Gift of Pastoral Love.

One day I asked Jason to describe for me his gift. "I actually feel the pain, the hurt and the joys of my people," he said. I can imagine that the emotions he has for his people are very similar to those felt by a mother for her children, a deep and abiding love carried inside that is almost beyond words to express. Jason loves his God-given gift, and so does his church family. I believe Pastor Jason will soon celebrate forty years of service at that same church. He and the members of his congregation are joined to each other in love. Love and enjoy your gift, and others will too.

CHAPTER 7

Your Gift Is an Expression of God

"What does God look like, Mommy?" Jeffrey asked. Most moms have heard that question at least once from their young children. When possible, they can always say, "Go ask your father." Of course, he may refer them back to Mom, who is supposed to be the carrier of all family wisdom. Don't dare tell anyone that assumption is false.

If you are a parent, what is your answer to that question? As a professional counselor, I have found that all of us, from early childhood, have wondered about God.

Now this is not a book on theology; it is a book on life and the gift God has placed inside of you. But most of us have some concept of God.

For each of us, our concept of God has been molded and influenced by life's experiences and by those caring persons around us. Who influenced your God concept? I hope their influence was positive and healthy.

Your gift is an expression of God. I am convinced that God is good and loving and just. Thus, it is easy for me to present God through my gift as such a person. While I do not pretend to fully understand all the good and the bad in life, I do know that God is love and God is the final Judge.

What's my point with all of this? It is that others see God through my gift. Like it or not, this is just real life. So be careful how you share that gift inside of you. Its influence is profound.

Traci is a dear friend who loves to travel. Her career requires her to travel a lot, so she combines work and fun on those trips. I like to think that God wants me to have as much fun in life as work. (Just a thought.)

Last year Traci was flying from the East Coast to the West Coast of America. She had settled back into that large, leather seat in first class with a good cup of coffee and her shoes off. The back of the plane was filling, and in a few minutes they would be airborne.

Then Traci heard a flight attendant say, "Look at all these soldiers boarding." Immediately, she had a God-given thought, and her gift followed into action. When she spotted a certain solider, her heart melted into tears, and she pleaded with the attendant, "Miss, please I need your help. I want to trade places on this flight with that soldier who has lost his left leg."

The flight attendant looked bewildered but said, "Okay," and they switched seats just as the plane began to taxi for takeoff. You see, my dear friend Traci has the Gift of Compassion.

Did Traci reflect God in that act of love? Oh, yes, I think she did. When she told me about this experience, I was overwhelmed with emotions of gratitude for a God who gives people such a lovely gift. Wouldn't you agree?

Our gift is expressed in a very practical manner. Traci told me about the look on that soldier's face, as he heard the attendant say, "You now have a seat in first class as a gift from someone." She also described how much she enjoyed that moment, her opportunity to love someone in a simple way.

Please do not underestimate the influence of your gift on other people. It might even change their view of God. What does God look like? God looks like your gift of love to another person. Someone around you today needs your gift of love to be given, and it may be their only reflection of a loving God they have ever had or ever will have in life.

If you are a person of faith, do you share it often enough? My world seems to be full of skeptics. People prefer to see faith in action rather than just hear about it. Does that sound familiar to you? I suggest that we show as well as tell. This is where your gift is so awesome. It is your best way to love others and to show God to them.

It's really easy to show someone love through your gift. It can be done through a simple momentary act of kindness. After all, every God-given gift is shared in love and compassion.

Have you ever been caught in a snow storm? It happened to me once. I was driving alone to another state to visit my parents and had planned to be at their house by dinner time. (Of course, no one cooks like my mother.) I had been planning the trip for weeks (planning is important, you know), and I thought I had it all worked out. Then, around midday I noticed a lot of low clouds moving in over my car, and I had an uneasy feeling. I decided to get an update on the weather from the radio. To my great surprise, the forecast was for heavy snow beginning by mid-afternoon.

Sure enough, the snow began to fall, and I was in a secluded section of the interstate. After two hours of snow driving (which I hate), I was still about twenty miles from my parents' home and I could no longer see the road in front of me.

I stopped at a country service station (where they still pump your gas and say "thank you"), and was surprised that such a place still existed. As I entered the old store and garage, I saw an elderly man whom I had known in the community as a child. His face was more full now and wrinkled, and there was very little hair adorning his head, but I recognized that it was Jack.

Back then I had known him as Mr. Simmons, but since we were now both adults, I felt that I could address him as Jack. He smiled at me and came over for a hug. It was a moment for two friends to reconnect after many years.

"Going to see your parents?" Jack asked.

"Well, I thought I was until all of this snow came my way," I replied with a smile.

Jack just grinned and said, "Guess you have become too much of a city dweller."

I didn't reply to that, but then he offered to help me. "Come on and get your stuff, and me and my old truck will take you the rest of the way home," he muttered as he picked up a set of keys from behind the counter.

Ignoring the torn seat covers, the lack of heat and the variety of smells in his old truck, I jumped into the seat beside him. It brought back a lot of memories of "the salt of the earth" people like Jack I had loved in childhood. He was still the man I had admired way back then.

You must know someone like Jack. They just always seem to be there when you need them. Thank God for the Jacks in life.

I saw God's love for me that afternoon reflected in Jack and his act of kindness. Sometimes we think that our gift has to be presented in a spectacular way. The only real requirement is that it be given to another at their moment of need.

How could you not love people like Jack? Jack died three years ago, and I traveled back over that same road and past his store to attend the funeral. This time it was sunny and warm out, with no snow forecast. God bless you, Jack, and thank you for helping me on that snowy afternoon. Your compassion was a shining gift to a weary and cold traveler. Your Gift of Helps reacquainted two friends and reminded me of God's care and abiding presence. Moments like those with Jack make life worthwhile.

Perhaps you have never felt that your life could honor God. I assure you that it can. You see, God has made each of us for that purpose. You were designed and gifted to honor the God of the Universe. For most people, it's done through just living life.

Capturing the moments and releasing your gift is honoring God. It may not make you rich and famous, but you will help someone in need, and they will forever be grateful for you and your gift.

Life is about serving others and honoring our Creator in the process. You will love your life beyond words as you learn to invest in others. Just be yourself and allow God to be seen through your gift.

Have you ever known someone who saw what others did not? Anna's parents noticed when she was only about four that she could draw and paint whatever she envisioned. This was not just a natural fascination or the passing interest of a toddler. Anna could draw like an adult who'd had advanced training.

Soon Anna was painting beautiful scenery. She saw a picture and then painted it to perfection. She has a version of the Gift of Vision. She is now nine, and her paintings sell for thousands of dollars worldwide. Does her gift express the Person of God? Of course it does, in a very beautiful manner.

Earlier this year I asked Anna how she felt about her gift. She said, "I see pictures in my mind, and I paint them. God speaks to me about what I paint."

Wow! That's amazing, isn't it. Whatever gift you may have, just express it back to God, like nine-year-old Anna does.

I suggest that our gift is an expression of God in the following ways:

Your Gift Is an Expression of God

1. Our gift is a natural, inner flow of who we are. It's not a learned ability or talent.
2. Our gift is a beautiful expression of God's love. It encourages and helps people in life.
3. Our gift is peaceful in content and in presentation. It calms the heart of anyone.
4. Our gift is freely given. It does not make demands on others.
5. Our gift openly honors God in some way. It may depict the beauty of creation or the smile on a child's face.
6. Our gift is well received. Most people appreciate the expression of the gift that you share.
7. Our gift is easily blended with the gift of others. It brings harmony and unity among other gifts.

These are only a few of the ways our gift is an expression of God.

Everyone wonders: Does my life really matter to anyone? The simple answer is, "Yes, it does." You see, the gift you carry inside is needed by many people around you. Chances are they could give to you examples of how your gift has helped them.

Unfortunately, too many of us tend to be silent on such things. It could be that your gift is so special that no one else shares it in your circle of friends except you. You may be more needed than you realize. And God gave you that gift for you to share. Your life does matter to many people.

I met an elderly gentleman back in the spring of this year. He was a guest speaker at a local church. Mr. Frank was in his eighties and had traveled the world helping people. He felt that God had called him to do so. I believe that he had the Gift of a Calling. In this case, a person is living out a divine calling. He or she may express it in many ways, but in every case the calling drives their life.

Before the night was over, Mr. Frank spoke personally with each of the three hundred of us who were present. I'm sure he must have been exhausted, but he felt called to encourage each of us in a personal way. The Gift of calling is another beautiful manner to express God to the world. Thank you, Mr. Frank, for I shall always remember that night and your gift to us.

When I was a child, someone told me: "If you don't use your gift from God, you will lose it." I suppose that could scare you into a submission at the age of four, but the fact is that God does not force or coerce us into the yielding of our gift. We always choose to do so or not.

Anything that's not freely given to God, dishonors the Creator. So, never feel pressured into a gift yielding. But, since God gave it to us, it does seem reasonable to give it back to the Giver.

My grandfather gave me a lovely gift when I was about five. It was an autumn afternoon, and the two of us were sitting by the creek in the woods behind his home.

Granddaddy was always creating something from wood, using an old but sharp pocket knife that he always carried in his front left pocket (along with some very flavorful chewing gum). We were listening to the water flow together and looking up into the tall trees (and I was enjoying two pieces of delicious grape chewing gum he had given me) when he began to whittle on a piece of wood.

I always felt safe and relaxed with Granddaddy. He was such a nice person. I watched now as a new creation began to take shape under his skilled hands.

I asked him what he was making, and he said, "I'm making you a walking stick." I wasn't sure what that was, but I just knew it had to be a good thing.

When Granddaddy was done, he presented the walking stick to me with a big grin. "Here is your new walking stick," he said.

I hugged him and remember how he smelled that day — like the woods — and I loved it. My grandfather had a version of the Gift of Creativity.

You must be asking yourself, "Where is the walking stick?" In fact, I am looking at it right now. Yes, I still have it. Could that be a grape-chewing-gum stain on the tip of it?

Grandfather's gift was an expression of God, and, as you might have noticed, it has had a prolonged, positive influence on my life. Whatever your gift is, please share it with family and friends. Trust me: God uses it more than you may be aware, and it becomes an expression of God's love and care for others, with lifelong results.

THE GIFT WITHIN YOU

Some of you may love Christmas as much as I do. Actually, I am listening to a mix of the season's best music right now. There are so many hurting and needy people visible this time of year. One night a man approached me for help just to get home, and the next day two more people asked me for money to buy food.

You may have experienced similar requests. I think the winter holidays find more people seeking some form of assistance from their fellowman than any other time of year. My thought that night and the next day was, "What do I really have to give them?" Of course most of us can provide some natural help for gas or food, but what else could I give? I suggest that I can always give to anyone at any time my gift.

Actually that's what I did that night and again the next day. Those needy people received my Gift of Encouragement and Love with as much gratitude as they did the money I gave. I trust that both were a good expression of God to them.

Michele has the Gift of Hospitality. She looks for people to help and brings them into her home. During the winter holidays she makes cloth angels (from dish cloths) and hot pads. If you are the creative, hospitable type, then you understand her. This is her God-given gift, and it helps many people in their moment of need.

Michele showed me some of her recent angels, and I was amazed. They were beautiful and a treasure to be desired. She is taking dozens of these into senior care facilities to give away to the lonely. Does her gift express God's love? It does, for all those who feel forgotten. I was reminded to give her some money to help make more of the angels. I do not have her gift, but I certainly do appreciate it. Give your gift too, and reflect God's love to someone in their season of need.

When I was a child my dad took his car for repairs to a man named Mr. Bruce. Mr. Bruce was a very different person within my childhood world, and my mother did not like for me to accompany Dad to Mr. Bruce's garage, but I was a curious child. His garage was dark, damp, very smelly and always in disarray. I had never seen such a place before. Of course, Dad was always near, and that made it safe for me.

On one particular Saturday afternoon, just after lunch, Dad announced, "Let's go see Mr. Bruce for an oil change on the old Buick." Never mind that I had on some good clothes; there was not enough time for a change. So out the door we went, and into that old car I climbed.

I had my place, just beside Dad, since Mom never went with us to the garage. I wondered why. Dad seemed to like Mr. Bruce, and that made everything okay.

As we entered a big door of Mr. Bruce's garage, he smiled and welcomed us as if we were long-lost relatives. I decided that I liked the place because he had a big black dog that I could nearly ride as a pretend pony. I never did.

Mr. Bruce looked like a giant completely covered in something oily, except for his eyes. "I've been changing oil all day," he said to Dad. All I knew was that he was a mess, and I did not dare touch him. Mother would never have understood if I had felt the urge to hug him.

Dad and I went next door for a cold drink and then quickly returned for some more stimulating chat. You never know what life lessons you might learn in such a place. Dad was talking to another patron, Mr. Hunter, so I kneeled down (without touching anything) and asked Mr. Bruce, "Why do you change the oil?"

"It's to help people," he said with a smile. So I continued with my hundred questions.

"Do you help a lot of people," I asked next.

"Yes I do," he said, "and some of them pay me for it." I wondered what he meant by this but was afraid to ask. Later Dad told me. It was not that some people didn't pay Mr. Bruce; it was that Mr. Bruce gave free oil changes to widows and single ladies. I liked the sound of that — even at five years of age. Mr. Bruce and I became friends that afternoon.

The moral of the story is simple: Anyone can use their gift to help another, and, in doing so, it is an expression of the love of God. Mr. Bruce had the Gift of Compassion. Please realize that your gift, too, is important and needed by someone.

I'm sure that such childhood moments have influenced me until now and continue to influence me. There are no requirements for sharing a God-given gift, except a willing heart and mind to do so. Your environment or your position in life is never a prohibiting factor.

Children share their gift so easily. There are no accumulated walls of fear or doubt built up in their minds to prevent the sharing. They are just themselves, as God made them. I am convinced that we adults can be the same, if we are willing. Just be you and allow God to express Himself through your gift.

CHAPTER 8

Your Gift and the Small Things of Life

My dad grew up during America's Great Depression of the 1930s. As a boy, he wanted a bicycle, but there was not enough money in the family of six children for such a luxury. So he just dreamed of it every Christmas.

A well-to-do family who lived at the end of the street had one son whose name was Marvin. For Christmas of 1932 Marvin received a new shiny red bicycle. It was the one with all the chrome and a horn attached to the handle bars.

Marvin and Dad were the same age and good friends. After breakfast on that Christmas morning, Marvin rode his new bike down the street to see Dad, who could hardly believe what he was seeing. Every boy wanted that bicycle, and now Marvin had one.

As Marvin and Dad stood in the backyard admiring the bicycle, Marvin said, "Jump on and ride it around the yard." It was a simple act of kindness between two childhood friends, but Dad never forgot that moment. Everyone can share the universal gift of love and kindness. It seems that God has deposited enough of it into us to be given freely to all.

A good friend of mine often reminds me and others, "It's the simple things of life that really matter." I must confess to you that, as an adult, I have often pondered buying dad a red chrome-covered bicycle, but he now seems to prefer the car for travel. Perhaps I should get him one anyway for this coming Christmas. It's those small things in life that we remember the most. They are our treasures of memory forever.

If you are a parent, ask your child what they treasure most from childhood. I bet it will be a small thing. When I was about ten, our family went to the beach for a week of vacation. I adored the ocean and would be planning out the trip for many weeks. I was always the first one on the beach – even before breakfast. For me being at the ocean was like a first love without the possibility of heartbreak. On Tuesday afternoon, Dad and I strolled down toward Johnny Mercer's Pier to have a chocolate ice cream cone. Yes, life was very good! Maybe you can recall such childhood times.

Dad and I were playing an arcade game and enjoying the moment when I saw something in his hand. It was an unusual quarter that he had received in change. Of course I just had to see it for myself, being the curious child that I was. Upon closer inspection, I could hardly believe what I was seeing. But there it was, a keepsake quarter minted in the previous century. "Perhaps I will be rich and famous," I thought.

Dad smiled and said, "Would you like the quarter?" Just that quick it was mine. And guess what? I still have it after all these years. "It's a small thing," you might say. I suppose, but I treasure that quarter because of the memories it represents and Dad's love for me then and now. It really is the small things in life that matter most.

When you share your heart and your gift, it becomes a treasure for someone. It may seem small to you, but the impact on them may be long and large.

I am reminded of a lady I knew as I was growing up. We attended a country church near our home. It was actually one of only a few churches in the area. All the families in the church were close and familiar to one another. As you may know, that can be good and bad at the same time. Mrs. Inez was our teacher.

Mrs. Inez was a tall, slender lady who had three children of her own. She taught the boys and the girls down in the basement of the church, which other adults avoided because of the noise. (I wondered if the adults were just afraid of the darkness in those basement corners. I stayed away from the corners too.)

One Sunday someone found a big spider in a corner of the basement. We just knew Mrs. Inez would protect us from such creatures. Her love for all of us was obvious in her big smile and in her gentle manners. Plus, she knew how to kill spiders.

Mrs. Inez taught us how to love and to share our heart with others. I'm not sure if she realized the impact her words, her touch and her heart had on us in those basement classes. I am sure that her gift, combined with an overflowing heart of love, infused itself into a room full of children, and I was one of them. I can still see and hear Mrs. Inez in my thoughts.

Several years ago I was Christmas shopping in the mall, and as I turned a corner, there was Mrs. Inez with her daughter. Fortunately I had with me plenty of tissues for such a memory moment. I told her how very much I treasured those basement classes and the influence she had on us as children. Of course it was a small thing to her, but it was a very big thing for me.

Please never feel that your gift is insignificant. Trust me: your gift matters a lot to someone. God gave you that gift for a reason, and as you share it in love, God multiplies it for the good of others.

It's like the biblical story of the boy who gave his small lunch to feed the large crowd. You are important to the people whom God has placed in your life. Give what you have from your heart, and the effect will be profound and long-term. Yes, life is about loving people and sharing what God has placed inside of you. Someone needs your gift today.

Tony and Dawn have two sons, and one of them is sixteen. Several months ago, Tony and David, the oldest son, went on a mission trip to Central America. They visited some very remote jungle tribes who'd had very little exposure to outsiders. Tony wanted to give David a perspective on life that he had not yet experienced in America. Personally I feel that everyone would benefit from such an opportunity to broaden their view of life.

The experience was life-changing for David. At first, he felt that he had little to offer those tribal people, except some clothes and basic medical items which the group had brought with them. When they returned home I asked David to describe for me the experience. He told me the following:

"They seemed to pull out of me a love and a gift that I had not known was in me. I have never felt such a compassion for others." Sometimes we don't know our gift until confronted with people in need. A crisis of need brings out of us a hidden compassion and an awareness of gifting.

David mentioned to me how the simple stories of his life in America had been captivating to the hearts of the tribal people. "They sat for hours listening to me, as I shared my life and friends," he commented. Those native people still lived in primitive conditions, without any modern conveniences, and storytelling was their evening television. For David, it was something simple, but it touched the people around him. We do not always realize the influence we carry in a given situation. God knows us and the effect of our love and our gift shared with another.

Here is a simple exercise to encourage you: Get yourself an inexpensive notebook and label it "The Small Things." Record in your notebook a daily list of several small things that you have given. Remember that these flow out of your gifting in love to help others.

The purpose of this exercise is to remind you that God loves others through you. There are no small things when they help someone in need. Your kind act may last a lifetime in the memory of some person. Life is a series of small events rolled into a number of years. What you do does matter for others.

As I write this, Christmas is just a few weeks away. I have many small, but cherished memories of my childhood Christmases. Each year about this time I remember who was responsible. Her name was Louise, but I called her Mom. She was a master at making Christmas special. It was all those little things that she naturally did that just made me love that season.

Mom's dad was a farmer, and her life had been a simple one, so I'm sure that she and her family found joy in the small, everyday moments and events. And, for me, it was the small things with her that I remember so well.

For example, it was those red and green sugar cookies that we would make together for the holiday. I would stir the dough, while she poured in the coloring from a little bottle. Like magic, those cookies became alive with a beautiful bright color.

Mom would lay the bright cookie dough on a sheet, as I took the cookie cutters out from a hidden drawer beside the oven. Soon that colorful dough would be transformed into reindeer, elves or even Santa Clauses. And ten minutes later we were sharing a warm cookie with a glass of cold milk. Life couldn't be much better than that moment.

Those are the memories that we cherish, simple as they were, yet profound, because Mom gave me her Gift of Peace and Love. And, yes, I saw God in Mom and felt His love for me in that kitchen. Thank you, Mom!

Most people in our lives are not famous or world-changers. They are just normal and content, living a quiet life. But they possess an awesome gift to share with humanity. However that gift may be expressed, it is important to someone.

Please do not assume that what you offer has no value. Trust me: it is very important and necessary for those near to you in life. The people who influenced my life were mostly average and unknown, but I never want to forget them or their contribution to my life. All of our accomplishments are partly due to the love and the gift of others to us, and I am thankful to God for each of them.

Kathy, a good friend of mine, is a local attorney. She is very good at her profession because she is such a caring person. That, in itself, is a wonderful gift. She has the Gift of Compassion, and this gift is so needed in a world where we all make mistakes. Some mistakes require you to seek legal help.

Recently I watched Kathy assist a client who had made a very human mistake. As a result, he was required to appear in County Court to answer for his error of judgment, and Kathy was present to represent him. I saw the love and the compassion of God at work in her. It was a beautiful moment to witness.

That client was guilty of a small crime, but he had a strong advocate, and the process took only a few minutes. During that time, the client was not alone, for Kathy represented him as if it were one of the most important cases of her career. Nothing is ever too small for your gift to apply. You and your gift are special for someone in need.

Most of us have benefited from the wisdom of our grandmothers. Here are some wisdom nuggets from several grandmothers concerning life's small things:

1. Listen first and speak last.
2. Others may know more than you do about it.
3. Love people more than they love you.
4. Just be you and like it.
5. Life is short and then it gets much longer.
6. Make a lot of friends.
7. Be a friend first to everyone.
8. Give away more than you keep.
9. Don't worry about what you cannot change.

10. Enjoy the moment and be happy with yourself.

These are simple truths, but they will last a lifetime. Share your gift with them in mind.

One of my most treasured things in life is a small notebook. Actually I have several of them which I have collected over the years. They are kept in a secure place where only God and I visit.

Would you like to know what's in those little notebooks? They record special moments that I have had with God. Many of those God moments involved other people, people whom I knew God had sent into my life for a specific reason. While my encounters with them were brief and simple, they have influenced my life to the present. Those small, momentary encounters shaped my values and my life direction.

Your Gift and the Small Things of Life

God uses the small things in life to guide us into a bigger picture of who we are becoming.

My dad taught us children about politeness by his example. I remember how he would allow others to go ahead of us in a line. He told us, "Be kind and considerate of others, and you will feel better for it." I admit that, as a child, I had my doubts about it. But it does work in building relationships with respect and mutual appreciation.

Politeness may be a small attribute, but it always produces a harvest of good and grace in us. For example, one day I was in line at a restaurant and in a hurry (like most of us are at lunch). When it finally came my turn to order, suddenly, over my right shoulder, someone blurted out rudely, "I'll take the lunch special for here."

I turned to look at the man, and there stood an oversized guy just waiting to see what I would respond. He was about three times my size and looked like he had anger issues. The girl behind the counter looked bewildered. What should I do? I said to him, "Sir, I'm next in line, but my dad taught me to be polite, so you can go ahead of me." This left the man speechless and shocked that I had not scolded him.

I found a seat and had started eating my lunch, when the girl from behind the counter came over and said to me, "Thank you for being kind and polite. That guy is always rude when he comes in to eat." Then she gave me an extra side dish. I know it was a small thing for me to be polite, but someone had noticed and said so.

Anyone can express a Gift of Kindness. Maybe even that rude man will have a change of heart. We can always pray so, can't we.

Children are so natural and transparent in relationships. Luke was the youngest child of three and was very artistic, even at the age of five. He could draw almost anything he saw. I was good friends with his parents, so I watched this gifted child as he grew.

Jennifer, one of Luke's first-grade friends developed leukemia, and the entire class came together to love and to support their sick classmate throughout that school year. Luke drew a picture of a beautiful, protective angel that he named Anna. Then he, along with his parents took the picture to the hospital.

Jennifer loved the picture and placed it at the end of her bed where she could see it each day. It brought her great hope and comfort. Since then, Luke has drawn many such pictures, but perhaps none of them have had such a profound effect on another person. God uses our gift in small ways to love and to help others in a moment of need. God can use your gift in such a manner too.

Some small events that may be linked with your gift are these:

1. They become life-altering moments for others.
2. They become God intervention moments for others.
3. They become a keepsake memory for others.
4. They become an important part in the development of others.

Please honor the small things that you give and those that you receive. They do become such a crucial part of us. Most of us will share our God-given gift in small moments of life. Maybe no one will ever know about it except you and the other person. Still, it could affect unborn generations by one person's decision.

Your gift has great influence for good. Just share it, and watch the good that it births in others.

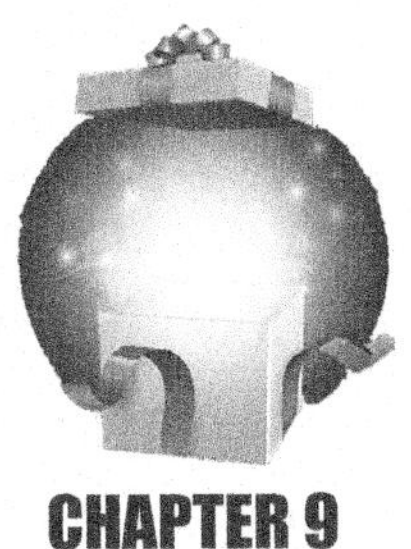

CHAPTER 9

Your Gift and God's Surprises

Life is full of surprises, especially in relationships. Occasionally I will reread a note I received years ago from a young lady I had counseled. We had completed a few sessions, and then she stopped coming, with no explanation. I wondered what had happened.

We humans are sometimes unpredictable. Perhaps five years passed, and then

I got this young lady's note in the mail. But there was no return address. She had written: "I'm sorry for having left with no follow-up with you. The truth is that you were helping me too much. I just couldn't accept the fact that I could be free after so many years of pain and remorse."

"Wow!" I thought, as I read her words. Sometimes your gift has surprises attached to it, when it involves others.

When I think I know everything about the gift God has given to me, I read that note. Yes, it still makes me smile and cry with appreciation for God's gift in my life. I suppose God and God's gifts in us are more diverse than we realize. I am very grateful for the gift, as well as for the Giver.

Such surprise moments remind me that even as a Ph.D. my knowledge is rather limited. Of course the gift in us is a God idea, and we just happen to be the blessed recipient. I'm convinced that there are God surprises attached to our gift.

Have you ever considered having your own blog or chat site? I'm assuming that most of you are familiar with them, but if you are not, find a grandchild to explain it to you. (Please don't be offended by that playful comment.) Personally, I cannot imagine life without the Internet. Can you?

My friend Sheri started her blog just for fun. It was a way to chat with other nice people in a safe environment. Guess what? Her gift (as is always the case) was obvious to everyone on her blog. They loved her and that Gift of Helps which she shared with them.

Sheri's blog has become so popular that she is considering using it to begin a new business. God and your gift birth new things that you have not even considered. Be creative and open to new expressions of your gift from God. Remember: the gift is for blessing humanity.

The expression of your gift has no limits. Don't place your gift in a box of thought, but keep it outside of even your perspectives.

I met Ann when my younger brother was in the hospital battling cancer. She had been a career woman with an exceptional Gift of Compassion. Then God redirected her and that amazing gift to become an angel to the sick. So Ann went back to school and became a registered nurse, and she asked to work with cancer patients.

I was sitting in my brother's hospital room when suddenly Ann entered with her bigger-than-life smile and this is what she said to my brother, "I am sent by God to care for you. This is my life calling. God has you here to help me fulfill His call on my life." The compassion in her voice and in her face was so breathtaking that I almost dropped my coffee cup.

Ann briefly told us her story, and I quickly took notes on my iPad, all the while thinking to myself, "What an awesome example of an out-of-the-box gift expression for a woman to make in mid-life. Ann turned out to be just the angel from God that my brother needed in that moment. Your gift expression will surprise even you.

Some people struggle with change. They are just fine, if their routine remains constant. Obviously, this can affect one's gift usage. I have observed, over years of interaction with diverse personalities, that anyone can change for the better — if they will to do so. (Don't get mad at me and stop reading. I am your friend. At least I want to be a friend and a kind voice to your life. So please stay with me.)

Change can be slow and in small steps, and actually, it usually is. I don't know about you, but it takes me a while to get comfortable with a new thing. A shift in how God uses your gift is slow and often progressive. So just relax if you are in a time of change with that gift of yours. It will be okay. I promise.

Stephen is a close friend whom I have known well for many years. His entire life has revolved around helping others in business and in pleasure. He, however, would describe himself as "just an average man."

Most people of Stephen's age would relax and prepare for the transition to retirement, but when I asked Stephen about slowing down, he responded, "Ha! Ha! Not me! I am actually in the middle of a major change of how God wants me to love others." Here was a man in his sixties who was embracing a change in his gift usage. Frankly Stephen surprised me that day, but then people do tend to surprise us on occasion, don't they?

Never be anxious when God births change in your life. God will prepare you for what is coming and love you through the process. Change will bless people with the gift you carry inside, so it's a good thing. Chill and be happy about it. Be flexible with God and how others may need your gift applied in their life situation.

When God redirects my gift usage, I always have an inner peace about it. Maybe the details make me a little anxious, but then I am just human. I prefer knowing the details instead of having to trust God for them. Can you relate to that? I thought you might.

God's surprises come in stages. There is a time of preparation for a coming change. This allows me to handle the shift. There is a moment of embracing the change in my gift application. I actually like the new idea that God has in mind for my gift. Really God just loves me gently into it.

Change is much easier when it comes softly. There is a delight in seeing the change. Suddenly you are watching your gift help others in a new manner, and you love it. It brings you a new joy and a feeling of purpose. It's as if you have entered into a new season of living. You wonder why God did not previously take your gift and love others in this new manner.

There is a natural rhythm that develops from the change. You begin to expect new results from your gift touching people in need. It simply becomes who you are. The stages are completed, and you love what God has done. God surprises with your gift are always good.

God may reveal to you an application of your gift years before it actually occurs. I know that sounds strange to many, but it does happen. Since God is the Gift-Giver, I propose that God has the right to do whatever in my life.

For some, the preparation stage seems to be longer. A friend of mine often quotes,

"The more God uses you, the longer God prepares you." Perhaps he is correct. Don't be discouraged if you are waiting on God. Just remember that God knows the why and how of all the circumstances being perfectly assembled into a completed picture. And, yes, you are in the center of the picture because of your gift.

Joni was born with an exceptional Gift of Communication, and she became an elementary school teacher. She was so good at it that she received many awards for teaching excellence, including some national honors.

Joni's parents had been missionaries to several Asian nations, and Joni loved those cultures. Her mom and dad were in Heaven now, but Joni had long wanted to return to teach the homeless children of those nations. As a single woman, however, she had been denied four times the governmental approval needed for entrance into her countries of choice, but she refused to give up the dream God had placed into her heart from childhood.

Finally, when she was forty-six, Joni got approval to use her teaching gift to help countless street children in the three Asian countries she so loved. Sometimes, for whatever reason or reasons, time passes before God shifts our gift application. The challenge for us is not to lose heart, but to remember that God will keep the promise to us.

Today Joni is one of the happiest people I know. She knew that one day God would fulfill her heart's desire, and now her gift is blessing countless children who have no other teacher. Now, that was worth the wait.

Malcolm was severely wounded during the Iraq War. His primary injuries were facial. Even his parents did not recognize him as he lay in a hospital bed. After many surgeries, Malcolm returned home, but his attempts to merge back into civilian life were traumatic. His days were filled with numerous stares from those who were shocked by his appearance. "Why would he be out in public?" muttered one person as they passed him.

Malcolm felt abandoned by everyone, except, of course, his parents and the medical staff at the local VA hospital. After seven months, he fell into an ongoing depression which required medication. He felt so hopeless.

A therapist at the VA facility was brokenhearted over Malcolm's condition and got him enrolled in a university course in which he did all the work online at home. Within five years Malcolm graduated with a bachelor's degree in psychology, and two years later he had earned his master's degree.

This true story has two amazing God surprises: Obviously, Malcolm's transition with his Gift of Compassion for the wounded is one of them. The therapist who had the Gift of Healing with his touch and his words is the other. Both experienced a God surprise with their gift, and the transition altered their lives for good. Today the two of them work together with the VA, helping wounded veterans merge back into life. God always has in mind wonderful changes in our gift usage for others.

My dad had five sisters. One of them I especially remember with fondness. She had a passion for change. For example, one never knew exactly what shade of dark hair she might have. I always wondered what she might look like as a blonde. I think she would have been a perfect character for a daytime soap opera. But then I was a kid, and no one ever asked for my opinion. (Life can seem so unfair when you're eight or nine years old.)

This aunt had a magical flare for colors, and it was not limited to her hair. I recall seeing an outfit she wore more than once. It rivaled a perfect summer rainbow in color diversity. Honestly, it was that bright.

What I recall most was my aunt's love for life and her willingness to be so expressive in it. That impressed me, even as a child. She was like a true child of the 1960s, in change and expression.

The reason I mention my dear aunt was to focus on her Gift of Creativity. She saw the world through different lenses. Life was not able to box her in. She was never just a black and white person. Please, those of you who are highly structured, don't be offended. We are who God made us to be. Nevertheless, that God-given gift you carry 24/7 can manifest itself in countless ways to help others.

That was the message my colorful aunt portrayed to me as a child. It was about who she was far more than just what she wore or how she looked. She said to me, "It's okay to just be you. Let your life be a creative gift for the world to enjoy." That was her heart, and now it's mine too.

A good friend is constantly reminding me that God is much broader in respect to our gifting than we might assume. I am sure that she is correct, for experience has often validated this conclusion. Your gift will take you to surprise places. For example, I just received a call from someone asking for my help because of her knowledge of my gift.

Recently, I was invited to the Caribbean to share my gift with many people in need. God will surprise you by opening doors of new opportunity for your gift to be given away. Just be available to the diversity that's attached to that gift inside of you. There are countless ways for your gift to show love to others.

I love the beach year round. There are so many different seashells on the shore. Some are in pieces, while a few are still whole. I'm told that there are an innumerable number of shells in the sea, and they are all different. We humans are all different too. Watch God surprise you in the many unique ways in which your gift can be shared.

Jasmine had a very disappointing experience with her gift when someone refused it, even though she had offered it to them in love. She felt deeply hurt and confused by this. "Why would they do this to me," she wondered. The experience hurt her so much that she refused to share her gift again. The years passed and Jasmine kept her gift hidden deep inside. "No one can ever hurt me again," she thought.

While attending a business conference with friends, Jasmine was approached by a nice gentleman who was the guest presenter for the evening. He looked at her and said, "I had prayed that you would be here tonight." Jasmine was left speechless and rather frightened by his words. She quickly turned and walked away, all the while pondering what had just happened.

She found a seat with her friends near the front of the auditorium, and when they asked her what was wrong, she told them what the man had said. Before long an usher came over and handed Jasmine a note from the gentleman. It read: "Please, would you and your friends join me after this event for dinner." They talked it over and decided to accept.

When the waiter seated everyone later for dinner, he positioned Jasmine beside the evening speaker. While they were waiting for the first course to be served, he leaned over to her and said, "I prayed to God that someone with your gift would be present tonight." He had recognized her gift and asked her to share it with him, and she did. For the next half hour Jasmine poured her gift into that dear man who was in need.

Even when we fail to recognize our gift, others around us see it. That evening Jasmine experienced an awakening in her gift, and that experience changed her life for the better. People need what you carry inside from God, so please share it with them.

Obviously, for Jasmine, that moment had been a surprise orchestrated by God. You cannot hide what God has placed inside of you. Remember: that gift was meant to be given away to help another person.

There is an indescribable sense of personal fulfillment that comes when a person shares their gift. Life's purpose is connected to that gift, and sharing it becomes the central focus of a person's life. It is the best they have to offer to a needy world, and it was God's idea for them to have it.

Life is a journey of revisiting the old and experiencing the new. All of God's surprises are good, including those surrounding your gift. God has you and your journey in control, so grow and embrace the God surprises that are coming for you. As you reflect on life, you'll see a master design woven together like a handmade quilt. It is a beautiful creation of God called *you*.

CHAPTER 10

The Priority of Heart-Speaking

Andrew was asked to speak to a convention audience with only a few hours of advance notice. The scheduled guest speaker had become ill and was taken to a local hospital. The audience was comprised of professional presenters, each an expert in their chosen field. Andrew was petrified by the thought of standing before such a group and having to deliver a flawless speech with essentially no preparation. What could he do?

"Speak from your heart, son," his grandfather had said. He was finishing a second cup of coffee and pondering what to do when he remembered his grandfather's words. Interestingly, Andrew's grandfather had been a country physician, as well as a farmer, during America's Great Depression of the 1930s. Andrew called him Grandpa, and he learned to listen when Grandpa spoke, for Grandpa was very wise in understanding life and people. Sometimes a life crisis will jog a memory from one's past. This was such a time for Andrew.

As Andrew was being introduced as the keynote speaker for the convention, he paused and prayed, "God, help me to speak from my heart like Grandpa said." Then, for almost an hour, Andrew held the attention of his prestigious audience. It was one of the most amazing presentations I have witnessed in my life. We all wondered how he had done it. What was Andrew's secret for such an unusual speech?

Later, over coffee, Andrew told me what he believed had happened. "I spoke from my heart more than just from my head," he whispered to me. It occurred to me, at that moment, that any God-given gift can be heart-given to anyone and with supernatural results.

This does not discount our accumulated knowledge, but accelerates it beyond just the natural. Is it a secret to be revealed? Can anyone experience it? Perhaps we Americans have so educated our minds that we have ignored our hearts. The impacting moments of life are more often heart ones than just head ones. Speak from the heart, and you will be shocked by the results from others, for we humans are heart-motived beings.

How does a person develop what I call the Priority of Heart-Speaking? The first step is to acknowledge its importance. If you are content speaking only from your natural accumulated knowledge, then speaking from the heart is not very important to you. For example, what do you remember most about your mother? Was it her heart for you or her actions toward you? Was it her touch or her daily routine? I am not discounting either the heart or the cognitive actions within our lives, only establishing a priority of importance within human relationships.

When we speak from the heart we speak into the hearts of other people. Heart-to-heart communication changes behavior and values in others. Heart-speaking then becomes extremely important and highly valued by the recipients. It transcends cognitive communication only. The first step in developing heart-speaking in your life is simply to acknowledge its importance.

The Priority of Heart-Speaking

Emily was in her first year of private practice as a pediatrician. She adored children, and they just loved being with her, even when they were sick. Emily had decided to open her medical practice in a small town in rural Iowa. She learned quickly that her patients wanted more from her than just the medical facts about their condition. They wanted to know her and who she was as a person.

I had the privilege of hearing Emily speak one day, and she told us, "I soon discovered that everyone wanted to know what was in my heart as a person. They needed me to develop the habit of speaking from my heart to their heart. This built trust and relationship with them and their families." As I sat and listened to Emily tell about her experiences, I knew that she had learned the secret of effectively giving her Gift of Healing to others.

Heart-speaking is craved by every age group and culture. The only barriers to it are those we erect around us as humans. I have observed that both men and women need more than just the facts. They need the heart of the matter.

A friend of mine describes heart-speaking as "communicating with another person's spirit." He feels that we can actually touch the eternal part of another person. Some people might call this "soul communication." It is more than just one mind sharing with another mind the facts and the information. Many world cultures believe that each of us has an eternal part in our being. Heart-speaking touches that eternal part in us. And, again, that's why it is so very important.

The second step in developing heart-speaking in your life is to pursue it. Years ago I heard a motivation speech entitled "How Big Is Your Want-To." The title intrigued me so much that I actually listened. I have heard so many speeches that a speaker has maybe two minutes to capture my interest. Are you like that too? This speaker focused for an hour on developing what we value in life. He said, "If something or someone is important to you, then you will pursue it." I suppose we all do this with various levels of intensity. What have you pursued in life?

Kathy and Mike were an obvious item in high school. She was the perfect ten and he was the perfect hunk. (What she saw in him I never did understand, but that's another matter.) It was their senior year in high school, as well as their third year of togetherness.

Mike assumed that Kathy knew she was to go with him to the prom, so he told all his buddies that he had her all wrapped up like a surprise gift, but he never formally asked her. Actions like that do not go unnoticed in the teen world, and once Kathy caught wind of Mike's attitude about it, things got ugly one day in fourth period study hall. A group of us saw the whole thing from the corner.

It was Kathy's finest moment, and we were all cheering for her. Not surprisingly, Mike never did get a prom date that year. What's important is what or who we pursue. You have a heart, so seek to speak from it.

The third step in developing heart-speaking in your life is simply to do it. God gave everyone this ability. It's inside of you, even if you have not yet developed it. Doing anything new just requires a beginning and a planned routine of practice. Anyone can master the art of speaking from their heart. Remember: the purpose is to enhance your effectiveness in sharing your God-given gift.

When you feel that you are ready to share from your heart, ask a good friend to listen. Prepare a brief talk on a favorite subject and ask them to be your audience. Then, listen to your friend describe how well you spoke to their heart. This is to be a learning moment, so don't expect to be perfect yet. Listen and learn from their remarks. Then maybe take them out for a good cup of coffee or tea as a thank-you.

Do you remember your favorite professor or teacher from college or from high school? Mine was a history professor in college. Sitting under his lectures for a year was a delightful experience. His passion for every class presentation kept us in awe of the subject. I am sure there was a waiting list of students for his classes.

This man spoke from the heart. It was as if the personalities from another time and place had come alive in those history lectures. Somehow he made it so real that we could see and hear what the people were experiencing. What an amazing communicator!

One day I asked this professor how he was able to make history come alive for us. He said, "It's all in my heart." It's easy to heart speak when your subject is heartfelt.

God communicates to us from the heart, so it's just natural that our gift would be heartfelt and heart-expressed. When someone shares from their heart, I remember their words.

I have sometimes imagined how fun it might be to play Santa's Helper at Christmas. (Don't laugh just yet.) I think it would be wonderful, just so that I could hear the sincere, heartfelt words of the children who come to speak with Santa. Some Christmases I have actually sat in the mall near the Santa booth and listened.

Children's wish-lists for Santa usually have items on them that have been pondered over for many weeks, and then it all flows out of their hearts in a few moments. Last Christmas I overheard one little girl ask for an extra doll for a friend whose dad had recently died. It took me ten minutes to regain my composure.

Make a decision that you will never lose your desire to heart-speak. Speaking from the heart releases your gift to heal and to encourage others.

Heart-speaking begins before words are ever used. You can communicate your gift to another without saying a single word. Gloria sets the atmosphere of her home for guests with a quiet Gift of Hospitality. You feel it the moment you enter the door of her home. It is powerful and draws everyone to her. She is one of those persons everyone loves. She knows the effect of speaking words that flow from her heart. Heart-speaking is a spiritual moment, as much as it is a natural one. God speaks to our heart before God speaks to our mind.

I have an older car that I drive often during the week. It's a fun car, and I have no payments on it. (No, it's not for sale.) Recently, I had a mechanical issue on the car that needed repair, so I asked a friend who sells cars where he would suggest having it repaired. He said, "Take it to David." He called David for me and told him I was coming over and to be nice to me. Good friends are like a priceless diamond; you keep them for a lifetime.

David had his garage business in an old warehouse hidden on a back street. After several attempts, I finally found the location. He was an excellent mechanic and very fair with his repair charge. You wouldn't want to have lunch at his place or even to wear a good pair of shoes there, but then it's a garage. (You know what I mean.)

Did you ever have a mechanic tell you the truth about a car repair? Well, when I went to get my car, after the repairs were complete, David said, "I didn't repair everything you believed was broken because some parts were still okay, so my bill is less than I had quoted you." I was speechless (it doesn't happen too often).

David had looked at me and spoken from his heart, and that made his words credible and his Gift of Helps real. Speaking from the heart touches the heart of others who hear.

So, whatever your gift from God is, let it flow from your heart. Anyone can speak from their heart. It's really a matter of choice: speaking from your heart or just uttering words from your mind.

Yes, I know that the heart and the mind are partners in communication, but the heart has to lead if the words are from one's spirit and soul. Your gift is an extension of your spirit.

My grandma would tell us as children, "Watch your words and where they come from." Heart-speaking is the most effective form of communication on earth.

Any person who speaks from their heart can recognize another who speaks from theirs too. I have thought how valuable it would be to have such persons in diplomatic positions. Imagine an organization that speaks from the heart before any words are heard? Of course that would depend on the people who make up the organization. Organizational leaders can sometimes be very wordy. Effective leaders speak from their heart and do not have to be wordy to be heard.

Heart-communication is simple and easily understood. A friend of mine says, "Heart communication works." That sums it up very well.

Your gift is spiritual in nature, so it's normal for it to be released from the heart. Life can manipulate us into solving issues with only our brains. Never forget that the heart is the central force behind life and directs the brain's decision process. Let your heart guide all of your thoughts and decisions, and let your God-given gift flow first through the heart. Others will love you for it and will be forever grateful. Heart-speaking is the priority of life in releasing your gift for others.

CHAPTER 11

From My Heart to Yours

Our lives are a gift from God to be shared with others. God has placed inside of you a gift to be out, and your gift is the best expression of your true self. As you release your gift into the lives of other people, you will experience the most perfect fulfillment. This is God revealing Himself through you to a needy world.

Our gift flows from our eternal spirit. While the release of it involves both the mind and the body, your gift from God is spiritual. As a Christian, I am convinced that God's Spirit births in us our individual gift. When we release the gift to help others, we reflect God's love for all people. It really is your best moment in life.

I pray that this book has stirred your interest to further pursue your God-given gift. My pursuit to understand our giftings has been life-long. Occasionally I am surprised by God's Spirit with new insights into releasing my gifting. Obviously only God knows the countless expressions of our gifting possible to others in need. Let's stay open and avoid closed boxes of thought. These can limit God's unique manner of loving others through our gift.

Keep growing in your gift understanding and expression by scheduling daily, personal time with God. Listen and learn to recognize the voice of God's Spirit within you as a Christian. Ask the Holy Spirit to guide you in your gift sharing. Since God gave to you your gift, He will certainly assist you in sharing it with the world.

Confirm your gift by the Word of God, the Bible. This book is written for everyone of all faiths. I am a Christian who believes that all gifts are from God. They are given to us through Jesus Christ, the Savior of the world.

Join with me in sharing your enthusiasm for your gift. You can influence others to discover their gift. Please remember: your gift is the perfect reflection of what God had in mind for you when you were born. Simply said, it's who you are. Please enjoy your life, and share that gift in you with others as you journey. May God bless you and love others through you wherever they may be in their life journey.

R. Lattier

Every desirable and beneficial gift comes out of heaven. The gifts are rivers of light cascading down from the Father of Light. There is nothing deceitful in God, nothing two-faced, nothing fickle.

James 1:17

Author Contact Page

You may contact Dr. R. Lattier at the following email addresses:

summerincity@gmail.com

or

ron@celebrationchurchnc.com

CPSIA information can be obtained at www.ICGtesting.com
Printed in the USA
LVOW04s0736220715

447156LV00001B/1/P